TORCHBEARERS
of SPIRITUALISM

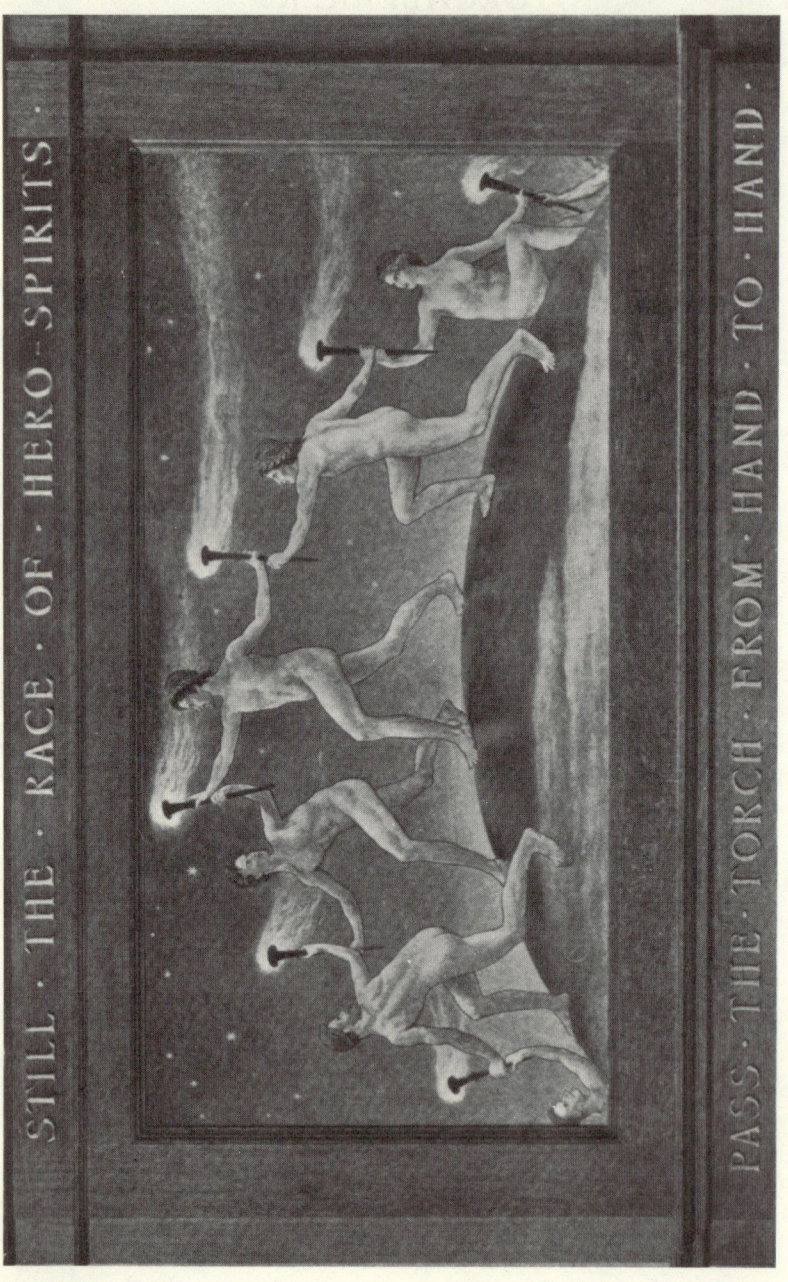

From the picture by *Walter Crane* in the Ethical Church, Bayswater, reproduced by kind permission of Dr. Stanton Coit

TORCHBEARERS OF SPIRITUALISM

BY

MRS. ST. CLAIR STOBART

KENNIKAT PRESS
Port Washington, N. Y./London

TORCHBEARERS OF SPIRITUALISM

First published in 1925
Reissued in 1971 by Kennikat Press
Library of Congress Catalog Card No: 70-118550
ISBN 0-8046-1175-0

Manufactured by Taylor Publishing Company   Dallas, Texas

FOREWORD

THE object of this book will be threefold :—
(*a*) To show that God has never left Himself without a Witness,[1] and that revelation has not been restricted, as the Churches assume, to the teachers, saints, and prophets mentioned in the Bible, but that the Torch of Divine Truth has been handed on continuously since primordial times, from one age to another, and from one country to another, and has never been extinguished.

It is necessary to draw attention to this fact because the modern Churches have done a great disservice to the religion which they profess. They have impaired the historic value of the Christ as a Witness of Divine Truth, by detaching Christianity from its chronological setting in the world-encircling crown of cosmic revelations ; and in their excessive zeal to magnify their Witness, they have isolated Jesus from historic continuity and from religious antecedents, and have presented Him as a Being supernatural and unique.

But in the firmament of religion, as elsewhere, there is no such thing as uniqueness. Stars and constellations are all linked, as interdependent units, in a gravitational whole, and it is only through comprehension of the greatness of the Whole, that we can truly appreciate the greatness of the units of which that Whole is composed.

And, for the reasoning mind, there is no such thing as supernaturalism ; the word is an abuse of language ; the laws of Nature are never suspended. Phenomena may be

[1] Acts of the Apostles xiv. 17.

for us unusual—that is, supernormal—because of our ignorance of the power of extension of our normal faculties, and the more wonderful the man, the more wonderful will seem to us his supernormal powers; but even God Himself would never stoop to break the laws of that universe which we call Nature.

The Christian Churches have, in short, lost all sense of historic proportion and of historic continuity. They almost assume that the religious history of mankind began with the Crucifixion, nineteen hundred odd years ago. All religion which cannot be traced in direct genealogical line from that event, has for them no value. The Churches talk as though until the year which is arbitrarily called the year One, God had been chiefly concerned in trying to hide things from us. If it were thus, He must have had some anxious moments during the lives of the great religious Teachers whom we shall discuss.

Psychic students, however, believe to-day that discovery of laws concerning the spirit-world, laws which are at the moment faintly adumbrated, is only a question of our own willingness to understand. That in fact, " There is nothing covered that shall not be revealed, and hid that shall not be known." (Matt. x. 26.) But we must make use of the means of discovery provided for us by the Deity.

Each science has its own special instrument for research. The psychic faculty is for the study of spirit, what the telescope is for the study of the stars. We might as well deny that the rings of Saturn can exist, because they are invisible to the physical eye and at the same time refuse to make use of the telescope, as deny the existence of the spirit-world, whilst refusing to make use of the psychic faculty. The psychic faculty is the telescope of the soul.

And the trouble is that in support of their non-Catholic ideas, the Churches proclaim doctrines which involve the infraction of vital laws of human existence. They preach the resurrection of the physical body, Virgin birth, and other violations of the laws of Nature. And since, owing to the requirements of modern science, reasoning men and women are unable to-day to believe in infractions of natural law, and in examples of isolated supernaturalism, the churches are empty, or are for the most part filled with those who conform without conviction, from social habit and convenience and because conformity is a hall-mark of social respectability.

The Churches crudely assume that for thousands of years—until the Christian era—mankind remained in spiritual darkness, unable to establish any relationship with God, and denied all knowledge of those great basic truths without which Man could never have oriented himself in the Universe, namely : the existence of a Universal Intelligence or God, the three-fold nature of man, body, soul, and spirit : and Immortality.

The Churches teach that—but for the Old Testament prophets—it was only " in the fullness of time," that is, in the year One A.D., the year selected by themselves as the beginning of religious history—it was only then, that for the first time in the annals of religion, God vouchsafed to send to Man a Witness of Divine Truth.

Even Moses and other prophets mentioned in the Bible are only noteworthy in so far as they may be considered to have been precursors of that One Witness. Such teaching is contrary to the teaching of history, it is contrary to truth, and it is desperately harmful to the Christianity of Christ. For a Church that teaches doctrines that are unconvincing, is worse than no Church at all, as doubts concerning the Church pass easily, as Eucken remarks, into doubts concerning religion. " The semblance of Truth prevents us from seeking the Truth."

(b) That the basic truths taught by God's Torchbearers in all countries and in all ages, though they have been variously clothed in accordance with the varying requirements of time and place, have always been the same ; and that they have been the same because they have all been obtained by " revelation " from the same source—the source of all true wisdom—the world of spirit.

But by the word revelation we shall not infer the employment of unique, or of supernatural powers; the word supernatural is, as we have seen, a misnomer, it is illogical in a universe which is controlled by natural laws. By revelation we shall mean communication from God and from spirits on the plane beyond, to men and women on this earth; communications conveyed by the only possible medium of intercourse between carnate and discarnate spirits—viz., the psychic faculty.

Now since mankind possesses this psychic faculty, it is natural and not supernatural to Man, and it is only legitimately called even supernormal because we have allowed it to fall into desuetude, and in this sense to become abnormal.

It will come to this: Either Revelation—in the sense indicated—is a phenomenon which has been experienced continually, in accordance with laws which though not generally understood, have been in operation from the beginning of Man's history, or no revelation, in the sense of communication from the world of spirit to the world of man, has ever taken place.

If no revelation from a God or gods to man has ever occurred, then the greatest intellects and the noblest characters of all time have cruelly led the world astray. They must either themselves have been fraudulent, or they have been the victims of their own imagination, and we are then—in default of any evidence of a beyond-world—driven to assume that there *is* no God, there *is* no Spirit, there *is* no future life—there is only some devilish force which has, for its own sardonic purpose intellectualized colloidal slime, called it Man, and fostered its aspirations of eternal life, only to stifle those aspirations in the eternal deadness of the tomb.

But if Revelation has occurred once, as the Churches admit, and as we believe, this must have been in accordance with natural law, and it will have occurred, as we shall hope to show, many times, under conditions in which there is, in all cases, a striking similitude.

But by what means have these Revelations come to pass, if all idea of supernaturalism is to be excluded? By means of the psychic faculty, and by the psychic faculty alone. It was by means of clairvoyance, clairaudience, divination, psychometry, materialization, dematerialization and the like, that teachers, saints, and prophets in all ages and in all countries received those revelations of Divine truths which they handed on to their disciples under the name of religion. And this leads us to our third assertion, namely,

(c) That these Teachers, Saints, and Prophets, these Witnesses of God, these Torchbearers of Divine Truths, became great Teachers because their psychic faculty put them in touch with the spirit-world, whence they derived their inspiration, their confidence, their mandates to go forth and preach their revelations to the world. Also because being in possession of psychic gifts, their teaching was accompanied by signs and wonders which even the ignorant could recognize as coming from a supernormal, though not supernatural source.

Again, these great Teachers spoke with unusual authority and exercised unusual power and influence because, owing to their personal psychic experiences, there could be for them no gainsaying the spiritual authenticity of their mandates. How could they who had seen with their own eyes, and heard with their own ears, and been in close communion with real, live, holy spirits, fail to speak convincingly of the truths revealed by those great spirits?

And conversely, we may ask, how can modern Ministers of the Churches, fail to speak unconvincingly of religion, of the birth, life, teaching, transfiguration, resurrection of their Saviour, when they have not even an elementary knowledge of the *modus operandi* of the laws controlling the revelations about which they preach? How indeed could these Church Ministers speak with power and with conviction on any subject dealing with religion when—according to their own belief—there is a chasm of nineteen hundred years between them and God-made-manifest?

"Mankind," it has been said, "has often paid for the realization of a great truth by temporarily losing grip of some other truth." Has not Man, in the process of realizing his intellectual faculty, the faculty by means of which he acquires knowledge of worldly things, lost grip of his psychic faculty, the faculty by means of which the divine Torchbearers acquired their wisdom of heavenly things?

Religion is, if we may judge by the religious teachers whose lives we shall here discuss, primarily experience, and only secondarily belief, and in supposing that belief must necessarily lead to experience, the Churches make their vital mistake. Experience must precede belief, for belief—so-called—without experience, is credulity.

We shall now humbly try to show that throughout all history, God has made use of the psychic faculty to reveal to Man those truths which the intellect can verify, but which, unaided by the psychic sense, it can never acquire; and that but for the existence of this faculty, which is the connecting link between spirit and matter, God and Man, there would have been no revelation, and therefore no religion. Religion is revelation. Revelation is the least common denominator of all religions. And if religion comes by revelation, men won't find religion by ignoring the only science which ever deals with revelation.

But assuming, as we do in this book, the existence of God, spirit, and an after-life, can Revelation teach us truths concerning these three great articles of our faith? Is such Truth accessible to us twentieth-century seekers after knowledge, or is it inaccessible? There is no third alternative.

Now it would be impossible to prove that Truth is inaccessible, till we had exhausted every possible method of gaining access to it. But if it is, as we believe, accessible, then presumably it would be by the great Initiates of the great religions of the world that such Truths will have been discerned. And our task will be to show that the key which opened the gates of Divine Truth for all the great Teachers of the world was the key of psychic science—a key which is as we believe available for the same purpose to-day, if we only choose to cleanse it from the rust of ages.

Pessimists complain that if there is a God, He is a callous and a cruel God because He has left us in ignorance of the fate, if any, that awaits us beyond the grave. But these pessimists should learn a lesson from the latest discoveries of Science, and realize that perhaps God has always broadcasted His revelations, and that it is we who have failed to attune our receivers—our psychic senses—to His higher vibrations.

Now it will of course be impossible within the limits here prescribed, to deal with more than a few members of that great band of Initiates who have, throughout the ages, understood how to set their receivers for messages from the fourth-dimensional world, and who have thus testified to the possibility of communication between carnate and discarnate spirits. We must content ourselves with choosing some of the outstanding personalities who have most clearly lighted their torches from the same sacred fire of Truth.

We shall begin before the times which in our parvenu schools and colleges are called historical, because whether these stories that have come down to us in the Sacred Books of the East, and which are now at last receiving the attention of scholars, are, or are not, historical in the strictest sense of the word, it is undoubted that we should never have heard of them but for their psychic content. And the psychic phenomena which formed the main features of these various stories, though occurring in widely different times and places, in epochs when there was no general means of communication, bear such striking resemblances not only to each other but to phenomena which are occurring in our world to-day, that it seems more reasonable to believe that the stories have endured and were recorded in the sacred books *on account of the psychic episodes which made them famous*, than it is to believe that these analogous stories emanating from widely divergent sources were in all cases the fruits—and there can be no exceptions—of fraud or of imagination.

How could primitive man conceive of the possibility of Spirit unless he had come in contact with discarnate entities ? A true mystical narrative is, says Mead, historical for all time.

Admittedly, however, our attitude of belief or of unbelief in the historic value of these stories will certainly be affected by our belief or unbelief in the possibility of psychic phenomena. Now we are not out to prove the existence of the occult faculty; belief in this faculty is as a rule a question of personal experience and of scientific experimentation; and the result of the world-wide experiences of many thousands of intelligent, trustworthy, and scientific people, can to-day be studied in many books and in many places. We shall only try to show that the revelation of all the Torchbearers whose lives we are about to sketch, has been obtained by means of the psychic faculty, and that revelation and the existence of this faculty must stand or fall together.

Those people, therefore, who disbelieve in the possibility of all psychic phenomena, must disbelieve in all revelations, and hence in all religions wheresoever these latter may have originated, since they were all, according to our showing, based upon supernormal occurrences—and this book is not for them.

But those who believe that under certain conditions, phenomena, similar in type to those recounted of the heroes of the world's religions, are occurring in our midst to-day, will probably be predisposed to give credence to the main outlines of stories which have come down to us on account of the psychic occurrences which made them famous.

And if we at all succeed in our purpose, such readers will then find justification for believing in spirit as the great medium of religion, and as the sole means of re-lighting the dying embers of Christianity. They will see that religion *is* revelation, that revelation is obtained by means of the psychic faculty, and that but for this sacred faculty there would have been no revelation and therefore no religion. Frederick Myers, the brave pioneer of psychic science, beautifully expressed this truth in his great classic *Human Personality, its Survival of Bodily Death*. He said, " In consequence of the new evidence, all reasoning men and women a century hence will believe the resurrection of Christ, whereas, in default of the new evidence, no reasoning men a century hence would have believed it."

We owe the facts contained in the first stories which we shall here present, to the indefatigable researches chiefly of Fabre d'Olivet, the great French esoteric metaphysician of the nineteenth century, to St. Yves d'Alveydres, and to Edouard Schuré.

D'Olivet was born in 1768, at Ganges in Bas-Languedoc, and he died in 1825. He first acquired a profound knowledge of the sciences, philosophies, literatures, and languages of the West, and then, in order that he might be enabled to penetrate the sacred mysteries of the fallen Sanctuaries, in those countries which were the great cradles of religion, he also acquired the Chinese, Sanscrit, Arabic, and Hebrew languages, and made a deep study of esoteric or religious science as revealed in the Sacred Books of the East—the archives which contain the first chapters of the history of the world.

He was therefore exceptionally well equipped for his great task. His book, *Hermeneutic Interpretation of the Origin of the Social State of Man and of the Destiny of the Adamic Race*—a forbidding title for a peculiarly fascinating volume—is a condensation of the history of the White or Borean Race—our race—which he traces across time and space. D'Olivet assures us that this beginning of history is a hypothesis only in relation to details, and that he could prove the substance by a great number of authorities, and even give the secular date for the principal events, and it is from this book and from *Mission des Juifs*, by St. Yves d'Alveydres, published in 1884, and also from *Les Grands Initiés*, by Edouard Schuré, that we have derived the

14 TORCHBEARERS OF SPIRITUALISM

substance of the following stories concerning the prehistoric Torchbearers of our race. We do not pretend to original research. We leave the responsibility for facts and statements in the capable hands of those who had a genius and a life-long equipment for the task; our concern will only be to derive deductions from those facts and statements. And in consideration of the purpose we have in view, we feel sure that M. Fabre d'Olivet, M. St. Yves d'Alveydres and M. Edouard Schuré will not grudge us the results of their researches.

CONTENTS

	PAGE
FOREWORD	5
VOLUSPA	17
RAMA	24
KRISHNA	35
ORPHEUS	43
HERMES	46
MOSES	49
PYTHAGORAS	58
THE BUDDHA	68
LAO-TZU	77
HERACLITUS	90
SOCRATES	93
PLATO	107
APOLLONIUS OF TYANA	115
PLOTINUS	129
MOHAMMED	136
JOAN OF ARC	149
ST. TERESA	160

16 TORCHBEARERS OF SPIRITUALISM

	PAGE
GEORGE FOX	174
SWEDENBORG	186
JOHN WESLEY	199
THE CHRIST	213
BIBLIOGRAPHY	230

Torchbearers of Spiritualism

VOLUSPA

(approximately 6,750 years B.C.*)* [1]

THE first of God's Witnesses of whom in the sacred books we have official record was, as we might expect, a woman, by name Voluspa, a name which means " One who sees the universality of things." She was not only for our race, the mother of religion as revealed to her by means of her psychic faculty, but the mother also through religion thus revealed, of music, rhythm, song, and grammar.

She belonged to the Borean Race, a white race, wanderers on the North-European steppes, a nomad people who called themselves Kelts or heroes, and who were given by their enemies, the black-skinned Sudeens or Atlanteans, the opprobrious name of Scythians, signifying spittle—something which repels.

Now it is clear from the caustic remarks made by D'Olivet throughout this book, that he was no lover of feminism. We may therefore assume that he has not gone out of his way to ransack the archives for this story which exalts a woman to a very high place in human history : but that the story forced itself upon him in his search for truth. And—as he gives it us—this is the account of the dawn of religion and of the first recognition of the psychic faculty in our Keltic Race.

In the days of which he speaks—approximately 6,750

[1] Fabre d'Olivet's *Hermeneutic Interpretation*, etc.

years before our era—men had no way of settling their differences except by force of arms, and the story opens on an occasion when two of the tribes had declared war upon each other. Their respective chiefs (Hermans) violently angry, had challenged one another to single combat. They had taken their places and already their weapons were gleaming in the sunlight. When suddenly a woman, all dishevelled, ran upon the scene, and at the risk of her life threw herself between the combatants.

With an imperious voice, she made them stay their blows, and listen to her. And though she was the wife of one and the sister of the other, they listened, for there was in her voice something unusual, something which to them was supernatural.

She told them that whilst in her wagon, overpowered with grief at the thought of this combat, she had felt herself about to swoon, but had not lost consciousness (an admirable description of the condition of semi-trance essential for the phenomena which ensued), when she heard a loud voice calling her by name. She looked up and saw beside her a warrior of colossal stature, encircled by a dazzling light.

He said to her : " Descend, Voluspa, gather up thy robe and hasten to the place where thy spouse and thy brother are about to shed Borean blood. Tell them that I, the first Herman, the first hero of their race, the Vanquisher of the Black People, have descended from the Palace of Clouds, where resides my Soul, to order them by thy voice to cease from this fratricidal combat. It is a ruse of the Black People which divides them. They are there hidden in the denseness of the forest. They await until death shall have destroyed the most valiant, to fall upon the rest and enrich themselves with their spoils. Dost thou not hear the cries of victory which they already shout at the feet of their idol ? Go ! Lose no time. Surprise them in the intoxication of their ferocious joy and strike them with death. My soul will tremble with joy at the sound of thy exploits. Carried on thy steps by the breath of the storm

I shall feel myself wielding again the strong lance and bathing it in the blood of the enemy."

The effect of Voluspa's inspired utterance was instantaneous. Her words rang true, and in this first story of our series we have an example of the fact to which we have already referred, namely, that those who receive their revelations directly from the spirit world, speak with an authority which none who hear them can gainsay.

The two warriors who had been on the point of murdering each other, immediately clasped hands and swore thenceforth to obey that great Herman, Vanquisher of the Black People, first Hero of their Race. They told their men-at-arms of the event that had just taken place, and transmitted to them their enthusiasm and their faith in the power of their invisible Chief.

With his name as their war-cry, the tribes carried out his commands; they surprised the camp of the Africans, whom they found in the attitude predicted by the prophetess; they precipitated themselves upon their unsuspecting enemy and massacred them in approved Old Testament style.

This barbarous injunction on the part of the Spirit-Chief may seem for those who have only an imperfect acquaintance with psychic matters proof that Voluspa's inspiration had not its origin in the Spirit-World. For did not this spirit speak with the same passion that had characterized him when on earth? But those who have studied psychic subjects will, on the contrary, realize that the ferocity of the injunction was the best possible proof of the identity of the Great Chief: for men's characters are not instantaneously, and by a miracle transformed on passing from one state of existence to another; and if his affections and his thoughts were still chained to the earth on which his people were struggling for a place in the Sun, his advance to a loftier state might well be indefinitely prolonged. Similarly at modern séances, it is often the inanity and the triviality of the communications, which afford the best proof of identity of those who have passed. Tennyson must have been well aware of this fact when he wrote of

Gawain : " Light was Gawain in life, and light in death is Gawain, for the ghost is as the man."

But after the massacre the Kelts returned in triumph, Voluspa at their head. In passing through the forest she was fatigued, and she stayed for a while to rest at the foot of a large oak.

Suddenly, though the wind was still, the foliage of the trees became mysteriously agitated, and Voluspa, seized with irrepressible emotion, stood up and cried out that she felt within her the spirit of Herman.

The men-at-arms assembled round her and listened whilst she spoke with a force that strangely impressed even the most savage of the soldiers ; their knees trembled, and they bowed down with respect. A holy terror penetrated them whilst the prophetess unrolled before them the future of their race. She saw them, the Kelts, as conquerors of their enemies, vanquishing the earth and trampling underfoot these Black People of whom they had long been the slaves. " Go," she said, finally, " valiant heroes, march to your glorious destinies, but forget not Herman, chief of men, and above all, respect Teut-tad [1] the Sublime, the Infinite, the Universal Father."

This was, says D'Olivet, the first oracle pronounced among the Boreans, and such was the first religious impression which they received.

Thus was revealed to them through the woman, Voluspa, by means of her powers of clairvoyance and clairaudience, the two great essential truths of all religion, namely, the existence of a God, and the survival after death of human consciousness—a survival which for most of us presupposes, though it does not prove, the immortality of the soul.

Voluspa became the model of all the pythonesses and of all the prophetesses who were known in the course of time in Europe as well as in Asia. Later, when the Kelts had become masters of the world, they raised for their pythonesses superb temples in substitution for the oak

---

[1] The Germans still call their country Deutschland—that is the land of Teut.

which, dating from the experience of Voluspa, became a sacred tree.

But from the moment of this demonstration of the prophetic, the psychic faculty in Voluspa, a stupendous change took place in the status of woman. D'Olivet tells us that at an earlier period woman had been the mistress and man the slave of the household, but that the female sex in foolishly pitting ruse against physical force had gradually and, as he thinks deservedly, lost their ascendancy. And at the period immediately preceding this sudden appearance of Voluspa, the lot of woman was deplorable. But dating from this event, women now took on a divine character in the eyes of men.

Hitherto humiliated, on account of their weakness which prevented them from sharing in the all-important work of fighting, they were now exalted on account of the new and marvellous faculty which was discovered in them, for other women besides Voluspa were found to have the faculty, and besides minor mediums, every tribe had its great prophetess who used to prophesy and divine under the shade of giant oak trees.

Thus, from having held the lowest place in the social scale, they were now all at once raised to the highest. They were regarded as interpreters of Heaven; they were declared law-makers; their orders were received as oracles. Invested with supreme sacerdotal power, they exercised the first theocracy amongst the Kelts. A college of women was entrusted to regulate all things in the cult of religion and in the government. In the different countries occupied by the Kelts several colleges for women were established, and at the head of each was a Druidess who was under the orders of Voluspa only.

These Druidesses presided over the cult and uttered the oracles; they were consulted on special affairs, as Voluspa was consulted on general affairs. The Druids did nothing without taking their advice and even the kings obeyed their orders.

But the results of Voluspa's prophetic gift were far-reaching in yet other fields. We are told that the prophetess delivered her oracles in measured phrases of regular form and that the tone in which she pronounced her sentences differed from that used in the ordinary language. The Druids took note of this, and by imitating her various intonations they succeeded in reproducing them and they then saw that they were harmoniously adjusted according to fixed rules. By hard work they reduced the rules to a system and derived therefrom those two most beautiful of all human conceptions, melody and rhythm, music and poetry.

And whereas formerly their only idea of music had been the noise of drums and horns and cymbals, now the flute was invented by some genius who discovered that with this instrument they could follow the voice of Voluspa and recall her words by the imitation and repetition of the sounds uttered by her. This rhythm was learnt by heart, chanted on all occasions, and taught to the children at an early age, and this made it easy for the text of the oracles of the great prophetess, which were always uttered in the same measure, to be spread amongst the people.

And for this reason we find that in antiquity, music, and poetry, which were never separated, were called the language of the gods.

But the divine art of Voluspa was responsible for yet another magical creation—that of systematizing speech by means of grammar. The Druids were led by the beauty of Voluspa's speech when giving her oracles, to study language, and thus they discovered with surprise that it was governed by fixed principles.

Needless to say, they soon found the necessity for using gender, and under the circumstances it is perhaps excusable that they should have pronounced the feminine gender to be first in importance. They, for instance, attributed to the Sun, the feminine gender, as appropriate to its greater glory, whilst the inferior Moon seemed to be better suited with masculinity. This, comments D'Olivet, was "one of those mistakes showing the animistic vanity of Woman." But we gather from his remarks on the subject, that if he had been in Voluspa's place he would probably have given us an example of one of those mistakes which show " the animistic vanity of Man."

We trust, however, that at least in psychic matters we have passed the stage of sex rivalry and antagonism so rampant in the early history of our race. The psychic faculty is a gift which God has bestowed upon men and upon women alike. " Upon thy young men and upon thy maidens will I pour out my Spirit," said the Lord.

The development of the gift—perhaps the greatest gift within our reach—depends not upon sex but upon individual character and environment, and inasmuch as those who are mediumistic attract as their inspirers, spirits of either sex with whom they may have affinity, it is of importance for the world's welfare that mediums of both sexes should seek revelations.

And this suggests the importance of special training and special environment for mediums. Only in the holiest surroundings and in the purest atmosphere is it possible to receive the holiest messages. It is no wonder that it was of old within the sacred atmosphere of the Sanctuaries that the revelations were worthy of being called Divine. Back-parlour training of mediums produces back-parlour mediums, drawing-room training produces drawing-room mediums. Only a lifelong initiation in the sacred temples of the Mysteries can produce spiritual teachers capable of receiving and of revealing knowledge of the highest truths from sources that are Divine.

And here we have presumably the reason why there are not to-day more great spiritual teachers and prophets; because though there are many men and women who possess psychic gifts, more or less in embryo, there are not many who, having the requisite occult faculties, have also the nobility and strength of character to undergo the difficult, dangerous, and lengthy period of initiation essential for the higher manifestations. It seems undoubted that these higher manifestations are reserved, as we shall see, for those who undergo the severest training—a training which is, alas, not available in Europe to-day.

RAMA

(approximately 6,700 years B.C.) [1]

IF up to this moment our women readers may have felt a secret satisfaction in belonging to the same sex as the first great prophetess, Voluspa, they must now return to their more usual and appropriate condition of humility.

For as the sacerdotal class became enlightened, and arts and sciences began to flourish independently, the influence of Voluspa and her Druidesses diminished, and their authority began to wane. Man—the male sex—had now begun to realize the magnitude of the feministic movement in which he had carelessly acquiesced, and he showed signs of reasserting himself. Women, therefore, obsessed—according to D'Olivet—by vanity and egotism, determined at all costs to maintain their supremacy, and they decided to rule by terror if not by truth. They therefore initiated a horrible cult of human sacrifices.

On the slightest pretext, the Druidesses demanded a messenger to go and visit the spirit-ancestors and carry to them news of their descendants; and such was the religious fervour which Voluspa was able to inspire, that the chosen victims congratulated each other when they were selected.

It was regarded as the most favourable sign when the King himself was called to this honour, and he was sacrificed in the midst of applause and shouts of joy from all the nation.

The fêtes at which these holocausts were offered were

[1] Fabre d'Olivet's *Hermeneutic Interpretation*.

celebrated every nine months, and for nine consecutive days nine victims a day were sacrificed.

Fortunate indeed was the Chief who was thrown headlong upon the lance of Herman-Seyl : nine times blessed were the nine children of Haquin whose throats were cut upon the altar of Thor : lucky he who was crushed between two stones : or she who was drowned in a whirlpool—for women themselves were not exempted from these honours : young virgins were buried alive or thrown into the rivers in honour of Freya ; and in the practice of Suttee we still see the lingering remnant of the custom of wives who followed their husbands to the tomb and there strangled themselves, or threw themselves upon the funeral pyre.

And since the Kelts had by now conquered the Atlanteans and were the Masters of Europe, and had even pushed their hordes as far as Africa, and threatened Egypt, the cult of human sacrifice was widespread.

Now this all sounds very dreadful, but was it more barbaric than are our own methods of sacrificing in modern war, millions of our noblest manhood, in addition to countless women and children—to the gods of Nationalism and Commercialism ?

However, two wrongs do not make one right ; and St. Paul knew what he was talking about, when he asserted that God does not leave himself without a Witness.

Accordingly, at this gloomy period in the early history of our race, God, having taught mankind by their own excesses what things they must avoid, now sent another messenger to bring men to a further stage in their knowledge of divine truths.

In the person of Rama, who is supposed to have lived about 6,700 years B.C., we find the next link in our unending chain of witnesses—witnesses to the reality of the spirit-world and to the possibility of communion with the world beyond.

As we learn from D'Olivet, Schuré, and St. Yves, this young priest, Rama, was of a very different type to the priests and prophets of his day, who had degenerated into being merely magicians of the black arts. He took his vocation seriously, and in addition to cultivating his psychic faculties, he made himself learned in all the arts and sciences of his day—astrology and the properties of plants, etc. Not content with this, but wishing to obtain a deeper insight into divine truths, he visited other countries to obtain from their wise men some of the higher secrets of occultism.

On his return to his own country—to Europe—he was horrified at the extent to which the cult of human sacrifice had spread, and when a plague (elephantiasis) broke out amongst the people, he took this to be a divine chastisement for their sacrilegious practices.

He was deeply distressed, and one day when in accordance with his custom he lay under the shade of a large oak to meditate, he fell asleep, pondering ways and means of dealing with the moral and physical evils all around him. But specially was he concerned as to what could be done to allay this devastating plague.

Suddenly he was awaked by hearing close beside him a loud voice calling him by name. He was surprised to see standing before him a tall, majestic figure, dressed like himself, in the white robe of the Druids, and wearing on his finger a ring round which a serpent was entwined. Rama, astonished, was on the point of asking the stranger the meaning of this serpent-ring, when the mysterious visitor took him by the hand, and bidding him arise, showed him upon the tree beneath which he lay a large branch of mistletoe.

"Oh, Rama," said the spirit-visitor, "the remedy you seek is here." He drew from his breast a little golden pruning knife, cut the branch, and murmuring a few words as to the method of treating the berry, he gave the branch to Rama and disappeared. The Spirit Intelligence was later known by the name of Æsculapius—the hope of salvation—and was regarded as the Genius of Medicine.

Rama was comforted, for he knew that here was the remedy he had sought. He at once made a preparation of the mistletoe in accordance with the instructions of his

RAMA

spirit-guide, and he gave thereof to sufferers from the plague, who immediately recovered.

The fame of the cure soon spread abroad, and Rama was everywhere hailed as a deliverer. He gave the prescription to the Sacerdotal College of the Druids, to guard as a precious secret, and his disciples, traversing the country with their branches of mistletoe, were everywhere regarded as divine messengers, and he himself, their master, as a demi-god.

This event gave origin to a new cult. Thenceforth the mistletoe became a sacred plant. Rama consecrated its memory by instituting the feast of New-heyl (new health), Noël, our Christmas, at the beginning of the year, and it is presumably to this psychic origin that we may trace our custom, not only of placing mistletoe in our houses at Christmas-time, but the custom also of celebrating, at the beginning of the year, a festival which was later transmogrified by the Churches into a Christian feast.

But Rama's Spirit-guide had further and more difficult work in store for him. Elected chief of all the priests, he was now told that he was to abolish human sacrifices. But the priests resisted this encroachment on their powers, and they proclaimed Rama to be a dangerous upstart.

Now what was Voluspa's attitude in this interesting crisis ? She dared not openly abuse him, so in public she praised him for the great service he had performed in providing a remedy for the plague, and she acknowledged his good intentions. But craftily, however, she took every opportunity to express regret that his gentle character rendered him incapable of rising to the austere height of the divine thoughts ; she hinted that indeed in this instance he even showed pusillanimity.

Ridicule followed close upon the heels of pity, and as majorities always resent, as being opposed to the Will of God, innovations that are contrary to current tradition, the Pythoness found many adherents. These maliciously softened the first letter of Rama's name from R. to L. and thus transmuted it from Ram, significant of strength, to Lam, indicative of a contemptible lack of power ; little guessing the sacred significance which would later be attached to this title.

But Rama's power was independent of epithets, and he was, Voluspa knew, a dangerous rival. She therefore determined to offer him the highest honour in her power. So one day during a great festival she summoned him to the foot of the altar. Rama, however, knew what this meant, and he declined the honour of submitting his head to the axes of the priest, and he disobeyed the order. He was accordingly anathematized, and now the only alternatives for him were to incite civil war or to expatriate himself.

And at this critical juncture, Rama was granted another and a wondrous revelation. The same great spirit who had appeared before, first gave him self-confidence by granting him an insight into truths beyond the reach of human knowledge, and then told him that the Divine Intelligence was satisfied with his work and that he was now to spread the light of truth upon the earth, and that he, the spirit, would be always near to help and guide him in emergency.

And it was upon this revelation that Rama founded his life's work. And what a work! Nothing less than the spiritualizing, the socializing, the civilizing, not only of his race—our race—our Aryan race—but of the world.

But he wisely realized that to do this effectively, he must initiate his new cult in a new country. So he discarded the alternative of civil war, and separating the sheep from the goats, he led his followers out of Europe into the heart of Asia, where he established a civilization which we, as descendants of that same Aryan race, are to-day vainly striving to re-attain.

From Persia he conquered India, defeating the highly civilized Sudeens or Atlanteans—the Black Races—in a mighty struggle, thus determining, as he knew, the future of the Borean Race, the triumph of his cult, and the question as to whether the empire of the world was to belong to the black or to the white races.

Tradition relates that under his flag fought some of the

Amazon or women-warrior tribes, also some of the savage Satyrs.

The war lasted for seven years and remarkable phenomena are said to have occurred through the operation of his psychic agency. In arid deserts, when his troops were parched with thirst he, like Moses, caused water to spring from the rocks at his command—possibly by means of the divining rod. Again, as with Moses, Heaven-sent manna was produced to appease the hunger of his people. When another, a different form of epidemic began its devastating course, he received again from his spirit-guide a remedy which arrested its ravages. This time he made use of the juice of a plant called hom.

Everywhere he maintained his authority and his prestige amongst people, priests, and monarchs, by means of his occult powers and his so-called miracles. He read thoughts, he foresaw the future, he healed the sick, all nature seemed to submit to him; in every word and action there was evident to all a something which was supernormal, and was then assumed to be supernatural.

Rama became, say the sacred books, the spiritual king of the earth. From the South to the North, from the Orient to the Occident, all Asia, Africa, and a portion of Europe submitted finally to the civil and religious laws initiated by Rama. He held spiritual sway over the Kings of Arabia, Chaldea, Siam, Japan, China, Persia, Turania, Caucasus, Plaksha, Egypt, Ethiopia, Libya, and all the colonies in the isles and coasts of the Mediterranean. His colossal wars are, together with his other great deeds, recounted in the Ramayan Valmiki, said to be the greatest poem in the world.

But he was no Hohenzollern, he conquered only to establish, never to destroy. With him *Vaincre c'est pardonner* and, according to St. Yves, he established on earth a millennium of peace and a government which lasted in its integrity for 3,200 years, and was the foundation of all that is best in our civilization to-day.

His government was a Theocracy in the broadest and

noblest conception of the word. Its principle was a Unity in which religion was the scientific basis and the apex of life. Its aim was the universal culture, amongst all peoples and all classes and in both sexes, of science and art, and of intellect generally ; and the development of Consciousness, a word which for most twentieth-century people has a painfully restricted meaning.

Rama, however, together with Initiates in all ages, recognized the existence within Man of a consciousness of a higher grade to that of the Intellect—a consciousness which puts men in touch with the spirit-world, as the normal, the intellectual consciousness of man puts him in relationship with the physical world ; a cosmic, a fourth-dimensional consciousness, which is probably nascent in all, though only as yet developed in the minority. In a word, Rama's Theocracy worked for the education, initiation, and selection of the best.

In the so-called Council of God, only the holiest and wisest and best instructed in religion and in the arts and sciences were eligible—by examination. And as a means of bringing the hierarchy of heaven, the science of the soul, within the intellectual reach of the multitude, he instituted the cult of ancestors, and thus he established a work-a-day connection between Heaven and earth, the living and the mis-called dead.

And everywhere in the State, as well as in the home, Rama recognized Woman, not only as the equal of Man, but in certain mystical, religious, and moral spheres she was regarded as his superior—in view of his treatment by Voluspa, a generous admission.

From Rama dates the saying which was repeated by Zoroastrians : " Le champ vaut plus que la semence ; la fille plus que le garçon, la vierge excelle l'adolescent, la femme l'homme ; la mère égale dix mille pères."

The Theocracy of Rama is, says St. Yves, clearly indicated in the sacred annals of the Hindus, Persians, Chinese, Egyptians, Hebrews, Phœnicians, Greeks, Etruscans, Druids, and Centic Bards, and in the songs of Ancient Scandinavia and in Iceland, and specially in the Ramayana, by Valmiki, and in the Dionysiaques, by Nonnus. And the religions of Egypt, Assyria, Syria, Persia, Greece, Etruria, Gaul, Spain, and Great Britain, were off-shoots of this universal religion of the great Initiate.

Other invaluable Runic records and precious MS. which would probably have given corroborative evidence of the existence of our great ancestor, have been ruthlessly destroyed by fanatics, as works of the devil.

But his influence was world-wide. He instituted, says St. Yves, Sybilline Colleges in all the Temples and in all the sacred towns of Europe and Asia. In Egypt every Pyramid had its learned prophet or prophetess, and in course of time there were Sybilline colleges even in Lyn-Dyn (London), in Ireland, Scotland, and the Isle of Man.

That these colleges were realities and not fictions of later imagination, is shown by the fact that they and the Sybilline art of divination are mentioned by such authors as—amongst many others—Aristotle, Plutarch, Pliny, Strabo, Ovid, Virgil, Heraclitus, Pausanias, Cicero, Tacitus, Suetonius, Eusebius, Diodorus of Sicily, St. Clement of Alexandria, St. Augustine, St. Jerome, St. Ambrose, Justine, etc., etc. But the books of the Sybilline prophecies were burnt in the times of Tarquin, and Scylla, and Honorius.

And we must remember that the words divination and prophecy did not merely mean that their possessors were able to foretell future events; the words had a larger significance and implied the psychic faculty in its universal sense.

And to the inevitable question, Why then, if this psychic sense was so widely recognized and practised in days of old, is it now derelict, must come the inevitable answer, that the psychic sense is a double gate which opens both to heaven and to hell; that the entrance to the latter is wide-mouthed and its denizens are always lurking ready to seek those whom they will devour; whereas, for communion with the higher-planed spirits years of self-sacrificing initiation are required.

For this reason it is essential that this great psychic power which is re-dawning on the world to-day should be shepherded as of old, by institutions dedicated to sacred ends—the Churches. If they refuse to re-light and to guard the sacred fires of living truth, on their heads will lie a vast responsibility. The study of psychic phenomena has to-day reached a point when it has become a science. Upon the Churches depends the issue, shall this be a science of magic and of black arts, or shall it be, as it was once, a sacred science—a science which puts man in direct touch with the Divine and shows him that he is not only a Son of Man, he is also indeed a Son of God.

St. Yves picks up for us faint echoes of Rama's greatness and universal influence in such words as Py-Ramide, Ramses, Ab-Ram, Rome, Ramadan, the great fête of Ram. In d-Rama and in the book of Job, chapter 32, verse 2. And after eighty-six centuries, we see, in the Lamas of Thibet, the residuary legatees of the ancient religion of the first "Lam of God."

But to return to the personal history of Rama. He became—owing to his occult powers and his wisdom obtained by means of his psychic revelations—the spiritual king of all the earth ; and then there came to him, as there comes to all those possessed of exceptional psychic faculties, the temptation to worldly greatness. He was offered supreme power, and here again his decision was guided by revelation from the spirit-world.

For one day, says Schuré, as he was meditating under the trees upon the offer that had been made him, Deva Nahousha, his spirit-guide, appeared, and told him that if he accepted the proffered crown, he, the spirit, would visit him no more. The choice was to be final.

Rama reflected for a moment, whilst the temptation, in the symbolic form of a beautiful woman, was realistically presented, then he made his great Renunciation ; and, as Christ later resisted similar temptations of the devil, so Rama resisted temptation to worldly joys and honours, and he retired with his brother Initiates to the mountains,

RAMA

whence he taught his chosen disciples the secrets he had learned, by psychic revelations, concerning this world and the next.

And St. Yves tells us that the sacred territory to which Rama retired as Sovereign Pontiff of the world was called Paradesa, and that it is from this word, with its suggestion of peace from worldly conflict, that has been derived our Paradise.

From his seclusion he continued to watch over his people. It was he who in his latter years fixed the Aryan Calendar, and it is to him that we owe the signs of the Zodiac.

No one knew when he died, and for centuries the people believed that their great prophet was still living, secluded, in his holy mountain.

Yes, it may be said, this is all very interesting, but how much of it can we legitimately believe?

St. Yves says that from various sources, and specially from the Sacred Books of the East, the history of this great Theocrat can be quite convincingly reconstructed.

And D'Olivet tells us that the story of Rama is only hypothetical in its details; in its main features it is steeped with truth. We ourselves have not had access to the sources of information at the disposal of these authorities, and we are in this book content to accept the statements of those better qualified to judge. But we may surely believe that there is no smoke without fire, and that there has never been a new religion or a new civilization without a great Teacher as the Initiator?

Also in those old days when means of communication were restricted, and notoriety could only be obtained by the performance of notable deeds, and not by cheap press advertisements, it must have required some noteworthy achievement to have secured for Rama the fame attributed to him in the Vedas, and in all the Sacred Books of the East.

In the Zend Avesta, Zoroaster—a rival prophet—yet designates him as the first man whom Ormuzd favoured with his inspiration. In Thibet, China, and Japan, and in vast regions of Tartary where the Lamaic Cult still lingers, he is known as the great Lama, the founder of this Cult.

By the Hindus he is still honoured under the name of Rama, and in the Pouranas, their sacred books, where are to be found the minutest details of his great works, he is definitely represented as a mighty Theocrat, law-giver, conqueror, founder of cities, and Initiate; and Schuré suggests that perhaps some day a closer and more sympathetic study of these wonderful books may yet provide us with an explanation of occult forces which the world is only now beginning to rediscover.

But whatever remains still to be discovered about the religion initiated by Rama, the basis of his teaching was, one Supreme and Universal Intelligence or God ; the immortality of the soul ; reincarnation ; the cult of the ancestor ; and the doctrine of the Eternal Feminine, in conjunction with the Eternal Masculine.

The Divine Unity was represented under the name of Wodh, but it was said to comprise the dual principle of male and female. I-Évê, Iswara-Pracriti, Osiris-Isis, etc., etc., the biological union to which the universe was said to owe its existence.

And now, from the standpoint of this book, we must ask, is it possible to believe at all in the existence of this great religious Teacher and forerunner of our Aryan civilization, without acknowledging that he owed his success as a teacher to his psychic faculty, which brought him in touch with the world of spirit, whence he derived his inspiration, his confidence, and his mandate to go forth and teach his revelations to the world ?

KRISHNA

(*approximately* 4,000 *years* B.C.)[1]

THE story of Krishna, the supposed founder of Brahmanism, as told by our authorities, is derived from the mythical story of the Vishnou-Pourana, and from the Bhagabadgita fragment of the great poem, the Mahabhârata—one of the most sacred books of the Brahmans, and from other Eastern sources.

Assuming that at the time these sacred books were written, there was some justification for general Brahmanic acquiescence in a belief in the existence of some great Initiate—founder of their faith—we have in Krishna, a fine illustration of our thesis that God does not leave Himself without a Witness.

The magnificent Empire of Rama, which included, as we have seen, India and the greater part of the known world, after remaining intact in all its glory during thirty-five centuries, was, in about the year 3200 B.C., in the throes of disintegration. And here we, who pride ourselves upon our modernity, are made to realize that we shall never be really modern until we re-become ancient; for this disintegration of Rama's great Empire was brought about by that which has seemed to us twentieth-century folks to be a special feature, for good or ill, of our modernity—the Woman Question.

And compared with the cataclysm which was caused by this eternal problem in the time of Krishna, our Votes for Women campaign was indeed a storm in a teacup. For in

[1] Fabre d'Olivet.

the year 3200 B.C. the point at issue was not merely whether half a dozen mortal women should be allowed to sit in Parliament; our prehistoric ancestors worked on no such Lilliputian scale. Heavenly as well as earthly etiquettes were involved in their conflict for the supremacy of sex.

The question which was started by the schism of Irshou, rival to the throne of his twin brother, Tarak'hya, was ostensibly as to whether, in acknowledging in the Deity Rama's dual principle, male and female, precedence at sacrifices and at worship should be given to Iswara or to Pacriti—to the male or to the female principle.

But there was more than this at stake. For during the course of the ages that had elapsed since Rama, sacerdotalism had fallen more and more into the hands of the men only, and the sacerdotal colleges and the Sovereign Pontiffs were quite willing to admit that in the Deity the male and female principles were One—provided that this One was male. They swallowed the female whole, and monopolized all the sacerdotal callings, duties, and privileges.

Irshou, therefore, who was an out-and-out feminist, reacted violently to this male aggression, and going to the other extreme demanded priority of place for the female, all along the line, from Heaven to hell, and the restoration to women of their sacerdotal colleges, their rights to the priesthood, and to the Pontificate, etc.

And now one section of the Empire, including the Hindus, held with Tarak'hya, that the male element must everywhere have control, in every sphere of life, in Heaven as on earth; whilst the other section, known as the Phœnician Shepherds, insisted upon similar rights for women. And in this cause three continents were soaked in blood and a Universal Empire was disrupted.

It was at this moment that, in justification of St. Paul's saying, there was born—among the shepherds, the adherents of the feminine principle—a great prophet whom the Brahmans even to-day regard as a divine man, one of the most brilliant manifestations of the Divinity—Krishna, the sacred one,

KRISHNA

Iézéus, the Saviour. He, seeing the deplorable condition to which the Indian Empire was reduced by the rival sections of the male and of the female cult, made it his mission to effect a reconciliation of ideas.

This he accomplished by a stroke of genius. He proclaimed that the two faculties, male and female, were equally essential and equally influential; but that they would remain eternally separated and consequently ineffective, if they were not united by a third faculty.

He thus established three principles of the universe, emanating from the Absolute and Ineffable Being Wodh, whom he regarded as inaccessible to human understanding. He named these Brahma, Vishnu, and Siva. This, says D'Olivet, was the origin of the Indian Trinity, which under different names and different emblems has been admitted or known by all the peoples of the earth.

Krishna then selected Vishnu as the chief Person of this Trinity, and he thus—inspired as we shall see from the spirit-world—reconciled the rival feminine and masculine cults, gave equality of rights to both sexes, in all spheres of life, and at the same time maintained the great central truth which had been taught both by Voluspa and by Rama, of one Supreme and Universal Deity.

Now with this story of Krishna, which is told in fascinating manner by Schuré, we, as Christians, are specially concerned, for the story of his birth and life bears a remarkable resemblance to that of the Saviour of the Christian world, and we are driven to suppose one of three things. Either the Christian writers borrowed the story of the main events of the life of Christ from the earlier legend concerning Krishna, or both were fictitious, or both had an independent foundation in fact. In this case, we may justifiably seek corroboration for the credibility of both stories, by searching for cumulative evidence derived from the tales concerning other great Teachers of religion in all ages and in all countries. This is our task.

There is not time to detail here the whole interesting story of Krishna, as related by Schuré in *Les Grands Initiés*.

We will restrict ourselves to those psychic events which are in remarkable manner paralleled by events in the life of Christ.

Firstly, His Birth.

His mother Devaki was, like Mary, a pure and holy Virgin, who, in accordance with prophecy, had been predestined for the sacred honour. And one day she was resting beneath the shade of a giant oak-tree, when she saw a wondrous light; the heavens opened, and from amidst a host of angels, the holiest of holy spirits, of dazzling radiance, overshadowed her, and she conceived the child who was to be the Son of God—the saviour of the world.

The Temptation.

As the devil offered Christ all the glories of the world if He would fall down and worship him—that is Evil personified—so the devil, in the form of a beautiful, artful, and wicked woman, offered Krishna kingship and the mastery of the world if he would love and worship her. Krishna, of course, resisted the temptation.

Teaching.

After years of initiation, Krishna, seated under the cedars of Mount Meron, started his work of teaching his disciples Truths inaccessible to those who are the slaves of the senses, Truths which he obtained by psychic revelations, namely, the Immortality of the Soul, its re-births, and its mystic union with God. He taught the triple nature of Man— body, soul, and spirit; that the Kingdom of Heaven is within us; in short, he taught, centuries before the Christian era, the same spiritually inspired truths that later fell from the lips of One whom to-day millions of people recognize as having had access to Divine Truth.

Transfiguration.

On more than one occasion, Krishna, whilst talking to his disciples of the radiant splendour of the One and only

KRISHNA

God, was transfigured before them, so that they, unable to bear the dazzling brightness of his countenance, prostrated themselves at his feet, " Indeed thou art the Son of God," they exclaimed—wondering why they had not discovered this before.

Sermon on the Mount.

Krishna first taught his disciples on Mount Meron, and then began his work of converting the people, in the villages, and on the borders of the lakes and rivers. Chiefly he taught that they must show charity to their neighbours ; they they must return good for evil ; that they must not shun the company of evil doers, as amongst the virtuous their example would be useless ; the Just must expect to suffer for the Unjust ; he who is humble of heart is beloved of God—he needs nothing else ; the Infinite alone can understand the Infinite ; God alone can understand God.

The Great Catch of Fishes.

The Great Catch of Fishes which broke the net of Christ's disciples is paralleled in the parable which Krishna told of a poor fisherman, who befriending a little starving child, was told by the latter to cast his net into the Ganges. He did so, and the net, on being brought to land, broke under the weight of fishes ; the child—a manifestation of the Divine—had disappeared.

Sympathy with Harlots.

Once when a woman, a harlot, was kissing Krishna's feet with her tears, the Rajahs asked him why he allowed such a woman to thus insult him, he replied : Leave her alone ; she knows better than you ; she has faith and love ; she is saved by these.

Krishna further told his disciples that the Son of God (himself) must die—pierced by an arrow—in order that the world might believe in him. Soon afterwards the prophecy was fulfilled, and he died, pierced by the arrows of his enemies, with words upon his lips almost identical with the last words of Christ upon the Cross. And—as in the Gospel story—the Heavens and the earth were convulsed at the moment that he passed.

Also again, as in the Gospel story, two faithful women were with him to the end. Indeed, when his body was burned, they threw themselves upon the flames to join their master, and the people saw the Son of God, and the two women, rise from the pyre in a cloud of light.

We thus have, says Schuré, the origin of Brahmanism. It would, of course, be easy to say that the whole story is only myth and legend accreted through the ages. But we must realize on the other hand that this religion of Brahmanism has, as Schuré reminds us, endured for thousands of years, that it has cradled a marvellous poetic literature, and several great philosophies, resisted the formidable attack of Buddhism, withstood Mongolian, Mahommedan, and English conquests, and preserved, even in its modern decadence, the sentiment of its loftiest and immemorial origin. Would a mere myth have had the dynamic force for all this?

Thus we see that at the fountain-head of every great religion there is always a great man, an inspired man, who derives his wisdom from supernormal sources. His work had a universal value, for his doctrines included two principles of fundamental importance for religion, and for esoteric philosophy, namely, the doctrine of the immortality of the soul and of progressive existences by reincarnation; and the doctrine corresponding to the idea of the Trinity.

We thus have a striking illustration of the fact that the basic truths taught by all the great Initiates are the same. Why are they the same? Because though these Initiates, these founders of religion, may be separated from each other by leagues of space and by centuries of time, they all derived their knowledge from the self-same source, the source of all true knowledge—the world of spirit.

KRISHNA

If it is true, as we believe, that religions do not found themselves, but that every great religion has its origin in the inspiration of some great Teacher, it is, on the whole, less difficult to believe that the founder of Brahmanism had an existence in fact, and possessed a personality which deeply impressed the age in which he lived, than it is to suppose that this religion of Brahmanism which has endured for centuries, triumphantly withstanding the shock of foreign invasions, and maintaining itself against the rivalries of other powerful religions, could have sprung into being by some process of spontaneous generation.

If then we may assume that Krishna was, to the people living in his Age, and to those who, within a few centuries of his death, inherited the traditions of his greatness, as real a personage, as was the Saviour of the Christian world to His contemporaries and immediate followers, can we not see that the missionary value of the spiritual experiences of both religious Teachers, and thus presumably of all religious Teachers, has diminished with the square of the distance which separates us from those Teachers, and that in due time, unless the experiences, the spiritual experiences of Christ can be corroborated—yes, even in minor measure tested—by modern knowledge, they will be of no more significance to the world of the future, than are to the world of to-day, the spiritual experiences of Krishna ?

Whereas if we can, even on a minor scale, corroborate, from scientific observations and experiments, the wonder-working experiences of Christ, we shall also be corroborating those of Krishna, of Rama, and of Voluspa, and—as we shall presently see—of all those subsequent Teachers who lighted their torches from the same celestial fire.

Thus the need for individual witnesses of outstanding character will always remain, for though Divine Revelations are easily recognizable, through all time, to those who have studied psychic science, they are only likely to be received by the multitude as universal truths, if they are exceptionally marvellous, and are identified with some exceptional personality who can be reverenced as beyond the taint of fraud, or worldly motive.

Hence the desirability, during the blank centuries, whilst there is, as now, no open vision, and no outstanding prophet, of keeping the Christian torch alight by corroboration and confirmation, however inadequate, of those psychic experiences which were the hall-mark of Christianity.

ORPHEUS

(*approximately* 1,300 *years* B.C.) [1]

BELIEF in the existence of Orpheus as an historic personage is not permitted in orthodox modern circles of the Learned. But since we are all allowed to believe in Pythagoras, and in Plato, as concrete human beings, we shall here accept their testimony and believe that they who were themselves Initiates and had access to sacred records not available for the majority, had adequate reasons for believing that Orpheus was, as they called him, a divine man.

We shall therefore accept the main facts as related by Schuré in *Les Grands Initiés*, and shall include Orpheus in our company of Torchbearers, asking our readers to bear in mind that our present purpose is to show that the psychic faculty has been the basis of influence of all the great religious teachers of the world ; and that in the case of Orpheus, the tradition that has survived is of psychic content, and that we may therefore not unreasonably conclude that this residuum which has withstood the attrition of the ages, was that portion of the story which had the most indelibly impressed itself upon the world as fact.

According then to the tale as beautifully told by Schuré, Orpheus, who was supposed to have lived about the same time as Moses, that is 1300 years B.C. and five centuries before Homer, was possessed of marvellous personal charm and beauty, as well as of occult gifts. And one day while still quite young, all the world at his feet, he suddenly, and

[1] Schuré's *Les Grands Initiés*, 125.

apparently unaccountably, left Greece and fled secretly to Samothrace and thence to Egypt, where he sought from the priest of Memphis initiation in the sacred and occult mysteries.

And the reason for this sudden determination of self-banishment from the joys of life brings the whole story marvellously up to date, and should appeal to many a man and woman for whom the tragedies of the war have served as an incitement to psychic study.

Now everyone knows the story of the love of Orpheus for Eurydice, whom he rescued from the clutches of the Bacchantes, and how these degenerate Thracian Druidesses, in their jealousy, poisoned Eurydice after she and Orpheus had enjoyed together only three months of happiness. But most of us have probably not realized that it was the death of Eurydice that incited Orpheus to abandon the pleasures of youth and give himself up to the study of psychic science, in order that he might learn how to get in touch with his beloved.

And he was not modern in his study of the subject. He did not suppose that he could master the mysteries of communication between two separate planes by a few sittings with a medium, nor did he suppose that much good would accrue to him or to the world at large by interchange of trivialities between himself and his spirit friends. Once assured, as he soon was, of the continued existence of his Eurydice, he probed to the uttermost depths those mysteries which are beyond the reach of the merely human consciousness. He underwent an initiation of the severest order, which lasted for twenty years, and only at the end of that time did he consider himself worthy of calling himself an Initiate, and of becoming a spiritual guide, capable of helping mankind to some of the wisdom which he had acquired at enormous personal risk and sacrifice.

He then returned to Greece, and was welcomed by the priests of the Sanctuary of Jupiter as a saviour, and by his science and his enthusiasm he carried the people with him, and transformed their religion, which had been corrupted

ORPHEUS

by the Bacchantes, who were then at the height of their degeneracy.

His influence soon penetrated all the Grecian Temples, and by his teaching of the sacred mysteries he formed the religious soul of his country. As the religious cults of all the great Teachers have been characterized by their personal proclivities, as well as by the requirements of the ages and countries in which they lived, the religion of Orpheus was coloured by his special sense of the artistic. It was through the love of art that Orpheus, who was himself a great musician, appealed to his Greek compatriots.

We all know the legend of Orpheus and his lute, and how by his wonderful music he is said to have charmed and tamed even the fiercest wild animals. But how many of us have ever heard of Orpheus as a great religious Teacher and Initiate?

It seems, however, that his power and his popularity were so great that he aroused the jealousy of governments. These, after a series of revolutions, forbade the reverencing of his name, burned his books, dispersed his disciples, and destroyed his temples.

Fortunately for the cause for which he stood, he died a martyr's death, murdered by Aglaonice, the chief priestess of the Bacchantes, whose exclusively feminine cult Orpheus had endeavoured to supplant by the dual—the male and female—principle of cosmogony. And this life-sacrifice assured for his name a lasting memory. Certainly to all occultists, Orpheus will remain for all time one of the great Initiates of the world. And since it was he who handed on the Torch of Truth to Pythagoras and to Plato—in whom we may believe as historic personages—Orpheus is an essential link in the chain which we are weaving.

HERMES

EGYPT was, as we all know, the great repository of religion, and of the occult sciences of antiquity. Within her sacred Temples, safely hidden from the vulgar, were preserved those ancient Mysteries—the life's blood of the religion of the great Initiates. And even when (about the year 2200 B.C.) Egypt was invaded by the Phœnicians, and her political independence compromised, the soul of Egypt was kept alive by a Brotherhood of Initiates, depositories of the ancient science, who safeguarded the occult mysteries from vulgarization, by means of a system of an Initiation of such severity that only the bravest dared to penetrate the inmost recesses of the esoteric doctrines.

And when the pendulum of religious thought swung from East to West, from Asia into Europe, it was from Egypt that the Prophets of the West—Orpheus and Pythagoras—derived their inspiration. Therefore, whether Hermes was historical, legendary, or merely a figure representative of Egyptian Initiates, and his name, like the word Buddha of generic origin, he must not be omitted from our series, as to him the Egyptians attributed forty-two books on occult science, and from the " Vision of Hermes," the centre and summation of Egyptian Initiation, and from the figured monuments, as also from the Jewish and Greek traditions, can be derived some notion of what was meant in those days by Initiation.

And when we read of the conception held by these ancient Seers as to the nature of man and of the education considered essential for Initiation into a wisdom that would

HERMES 47

lead to his highest development, the comparison with our own paltry pretence at education, is, to say the least, disconcerting, and we realize that in discarding, or in ignoring the sacred literature of the East, we have thrown away the best part of our human heritage.

For in their education, the old Initiates took into account the three-fold nature of man—body, which included intellect; soul, concerned with the psychic faculties; and spirit, the true Self which works through soul and body. With these Initiates, science, religion, and a philosophy of life, were interdependent. To them would have seemed childish the attitude of our scientists, including doctors of medicine, who ignore soul and spirit, and of our clergy, who ignore science.

Initiation was a gradual training of the whole human being; Will, Reason, and Intuition must all be developed simultaneously. It was believed that by deep study and constant application, man could develop his faculties to incalculable limits, and put himself in touch with the occult forces of the Universe. The soul has latent senses and Initiation awakens these.

But only he who can command himself, can command others. True Initiation was thus something more than a mere manifestation of psychic force, and a performance of conjuring tricks. It involved a knowledge of such sciences as were then available, the science of minerals and of plants; of the history of Man and of people; of medicine, architecture, and sacred music. During a long apprenticeship the Initiate must not only know, he must become.

He, the initiate, was left much to himself by his teachers. To all his questions, they would reply, not wait and see, but wait and work, or wait and obey. To the eager question, Shall I some day see the light of Osiris? would come the answer, "That does not depend upon us. Truth is not given; one finds it in oneself, or one never finds it. We cannot make an adept of you, you must make one of yourself. The lotus grows for a long time under the water before blooming. Do not hasten the unfolding of the

48 TORCHBEARERS OF SPIRITUALISM

divine flower. If it is to come, it will come one day. Work and pray."

None of these old Initiates believed with our modern theologians, that the world was created in six solar days by a caprice of the Almighty. They believed that it was created knowledgeably and gradually, by means of emanation and evolution.

And the knowledge of these ancient Seers, which embraced the history of the Universe, was obtained, not only from worldly study, but from the highest sources, after years of preparation. But on the completion of an Initiation which lasted sometimes for twenty years, and included hardships which few moderns would undergo to-day, the adept was obliged to swear, under penalty of death, never to reveal the secrets of Osiris, except under the three-fold veil of mythology, symbols, and the lesser mysteries.

And mankind to-day, instead of trying to rediscover the realities for which the ancient symbols stood, prefers to reject even the symbols, and to throw away a priceless heritage of heavenly wisdom.

Thus the esoteric teaching of these Egyptian Mystics and their esoteric monotheism remained within the sacred temples.

MOSES

(*approximately* 1,300 *years* B.C.) [1]

It was Moses, the Egyptian Initiate, and Priest of Osiris, who brought the principle of Monotheism out of the esoteric darkness of the temples, into the exoteric light of history. But in handling the story of Moses, we are no longer dealing with the sacred books of other countries, with books which our Churches either ignore, or at which they may glance in moments of literary curiosity; we are dealing with the story which is chronicled in our own sacred Book, a story which the Churches have engrafted on to the main stem of Christianity, as an integral feature of the religion which they teach.

But owing to general ignorance of the history of the world during Mosaic and pre-Mosaic times—an ignorance due to failure to study the sacred books of other lands—the true justification for the inclusion of Moses in the Christian Hierarchy is never disclosed; with the result that failing, in this instance, as in others, to obtain adequate reasons for the beliefs enjoined by the Churches, thinking people have no alternative to unbelief—and they become agnostics.

For the story of Moses, as taught by those for whom religious history begins in the year one A.D., for those who have no insight into universal history, and who have no knowledge of psychic science, is a tale of nonsense, for nursery days. Isolated and detached from all cultural atmosphere, and historic antecedents, and with its super-

[1] Schuré's *Les Grands Initiés*, 125.

normal wonders unexplained, the Mosaic legend has no intrinsic value for the Christian world. It is only when we glimpse the historic and religious environment which was the heritage of Moses; when we learn something of the learned and scientific atmosphere in which he was brought up, and of the religion of the great Initiates who were his cosmic predecessors, that we can sense the true status, in world-history, of one of the greatest psychics, one of the greatest Initiates of all time.

Then, read by the light of a larger knowledge, the story of Moses is a story not for Christians only, or for Jews only, but for all mankind. For it was Moses who gave to the world at large—through the mediumship of the Hebrew people—the religious truths which had been the jealously guarded secrets of the temples. And it was, we believe, and as we shall try to show, Moses who, in the first book of the Old Testament, conveyed to mankind, the most ancient traditions of our earth; traditions reaching beyond the epoch of the primitive Atlanteans, and beyond the catastrophe of the great deluge of which these people were the victims; traditions attaching to cosmogonical subjects of the first importance, to the first principles of all things —traditions of a wisdom derived at first hand by the great Initiates who were his predecessors.

But who and what was Moses? He was not a Jew, but the natural, or—as she would probably have preferred to call him—the adopted son of the Princess Royal, sister of King Ramses II. Of a religious temperament, and with exceptional psychic faculties, he was brought up in the Temple, and was deeply initiated in the esoteric science of Egypt. This fact was recognized by—amongst others— Philo, and by Clement of Alexandria, as well as by St. Stephen, who in the Acts of the Apostles, 7th chapter, 27th verse, reminds his hearers that " Moses was instructed in all the wisdom of the Egyptians, and he was mighty in his words and works." Indeed, without this special training Moses' work would have been impossible.

MOSES

And we must remember that a high state of civilization existed in the Eastern world generally in those days. As described by Ctesias, Clitarque, Herodotus, Aristotle, and Diodorus, the Babylon built by that great and beautiful woman-conqueror Semiramis, who was priestess for a college of women Initiates, a Joan of Arc on an imperial scale, the object of the enthusiastic admiration of the feminine faculty of her day, and Empress of Assyria, with a genius for government which is said to have surpassed that of all previous governors—this Babylon was large enough to have contained four of our Londons.

And it was not only in physical dimensions a gigantic metropolis, constructed by architects and engineers who seem to have been in no way inferior to those of our own day, it was also a centre of learning, and of sciences both exoteric and esoteric.

The ancients in the days preceding Moses, are said to have possessed a knowledge not only of astronomy, astrology, optics, pyrotechnics, accoustics, the compass, music, architecture, and anthropology. They made use of telescopes, microscopes, the telegraph, chemistry, organic and inorganic, and chemistry even applied to photography, and electricity. They must have had the use of firearms, as the use of these weapons of destruction was restricted to the sages of the temples.

Plato, who was himself, as we shall see, initiated in the sacred mysteries, tells us that a complete civilization existed in Egypt 10,000 years before Mènes, and the date of Mènes was 5,000 years before Christ.

Indeed Egypt, by universal acknowledgment, transcended all other lands for its accumulated store of wisdom, and the temples were the repositories of this wisdom. Therefore Moses, who was brought up in the Temple, amongst the learned priests and Initiates, had at his disposal all the sciences, both secular and sacred, exoteric and esoteric, and all the knowledge of the known world.

His library included the Encyclopedia Abramide of

Chaldea, the Hermetic libraries of Egypt and of Ethiopia, the forty-two books on occult science by Hermes relating to the social and divine Synthesis, which were carried in the ceremonies; he had, in fact, according to Manéthon, 37,000 volumes dealing with sacred science, and sacred science included in those days, as we have seen, every branch of physical as well as of religious science.

And if Moses was as highly cultured and as well informed as would be consistent with his education and up-bringing, and if he was as great and wonderful a man as his success in the difficult task he undertook would warrant us in believing, is it reasonable to suppose that the book of Genesis has no other meaning than that which is taught in our Sunday Schools? Is it not more reasonable to assume that, as was the habit with all esoteric writers, the inner meaning, though cipherable for the elect, was by the author generalized for the majority.

And that this was the course pursued by the author of Genesis is made plain by Fabre d'Olivet, who in the second volume of his valuable book *La Langue Hébraique*, gives us a literal translation, into both French and English, of the first ten chapters of Genesis, taken not from the Greek and already perverted text, but from the original and ancient Hebrew dialect, which was a branch of the Egyptian language. Thus even we, who are unlearned in such matters, can see and judge for ourselves whether it is not the translators, the transcribers, and finally the Churches who have made of the stories of Adam and Eve, of the Fall, of Noah, etc., a tissue of impossible tales, by converting the universal into the individual, the spiritual into the material. From this translation, he who runs may then read and understand that the cosmogony that is there presented in those first ten chapters must, when understood in the true and esoteric sense of the original, have been the result of wisdom which could only have come from divine, from spirit inspiration, partly to Moses himself, and partly to his great predecessors who had treasured their revelations in the temples of Memphis and of Thebes.

And surely if we believe that this great man Moses was brought up amongst the most learned adepts, with a deep and intimate knowledge of all science, natural and physical, as well as esoteric; of religion, philosophy, and cosmic wisdom, we can scarcely suppose that he would have concerned himself with writing about talking-serpents, and pillars of salt, and other similar absurdities—as *things in themselves*. Are we not forced to believe that Moses followed the rule universally practised of old by those who wrote on sacred subjects and who dealt with esoteric science and heavenly wisdom, and that he hid behind a triple veil, the inner, the esoteric meaning of his revelations? He hid from the vulgar in parabolic language the great truths he wished to reveal, as all the great Teachers have always done.

And that the first five books of the Old Testament were written by one who had a library at his command, is shown by the references to various books consulted. The writer mentions, for instance:—

> The Book of the Generations of Adam (Gen. v. 1).
> Book of the Wars of the Lord (Num. xxi. 14).
> Book of Proverbs (Num. xxi. 27).
> Wars of Jehovah.
> The Book of Jashar (Joshua x. 13).

And so, if we look to the Bible for Religion, and to the beginning of the Bible for the beginning of religion, we shall now be led to realize that religion is not born, as is so often supposed, of ignorance, but of wisdom derived from the highest source.

It is only upon such—and to our mind more reasonable supposition—that the story of Moses can be taken seriously. And if we thus take it seriously, and if we then as the next stage in our apprisement of the worth of Moses, can see in these first chapters of Genesis, esoteric revelations veiled in hieroglyphic language, we are brought to realize that such a composition as the Pentateuch *necessitated* an author of no less exalted a type than Moses.

Briefly the circular argument will be as follows: If Moses was brought up in the Egyptian temples, as is now generally admitted, and at a time when an advanced state of science, esoteric and otherwise, was in sacerdotal keeping; and if he was a great man, as we may assume from the acknowledgment of his greatness, still prevalent in the time of Christ; and if he wrote the book of Genesis—then the first ten chapters of that book must carry some more erudite meaning than is ascribed to them by our Church teaching. And if this meaning is cosmogonical and not merely chimerical, then he who wrote them must have had an intimate knowledge of esoteric truths acquired by occult means—and such knowledge presupposes a prophet and Initiate. And for this rôle, who could more appropriately be suggested than Moses? Those first chapters of Genesis, in short, " pre-suppose a Moses, as the *Iliad* and the *Odyssey* pre-suppose a Homer."

If then Moses was responsible for the book of Genesis, with its esoterically veiled Cosmogony, we cannot doubt that he was a sage of sages, an Initiate of Initiates, worthy of a higher place in religious history than is usually accorded to him. We cannot then doubt that the signs and wonders attributed to him were not merely the tricks of a clever conjuror, but a demonstration of psychic power on a scale which has seldom been equalled in the history of mankind. With the signs and wonders of Moses, and with his work, we shall not here deal, as we have discussed these elsewhere.[1] We will only now briefly record the circumstances, and suggest the conditions which immediately led up to the inauguration of Moses as a Leader of men.

Now we cannot doubt that, brought up in the devout atmosphere of the Sanctuary, Moses, with his religious bent of mind, must have been deeply distressed by the state of sensuous luxury and the religious and social degeneration which had followed in the wake of an era of political conquest.

For the era of Theocracy of the " good old days " had

[1] *Ancient Lights.* Kegan Paul.

been broken up by Ninus (Nimrod), the first political conqueror and tyrant, and first adversary of the reign of God on earth. And all around Moses, graven on the granite of the Pyramids, were proofs reminding him of the reign of God which had existed in the Past. He must have longed for the advent of a Prophet worthy of the great Initiates whose names and histories were treasured in the sacred temples; for the advent of one who would be able to keep alight, and for all men to profit by, the Torch of Truth which now only flickered faintly from within the dark recesses of the sanctuaries. And though he could never have foreseen that he himself, with his frail frame and stammering tongue, would have been chosen to play this exalted rôle, Providence has a way of preparing the stage for a great drama, without warning the chief actors of His methods. And so, by ways that seemed to be circumlocutory, Moses was, step by step, led on and prepared for his great work—in the following manner :—

Now the priests of Osiris, who committed a murder, were severely judged by the Sacerdotal College. So when Moses killed the Egyptian who was ill-treating one of the children of Israel, he knew that his life hung upon a thread, especially as the King suspected in him a rival to the throne, and he therefore exiled himself and determined to make expiation for his crime.

So he fled to Midian, at the head of the Red Sea, where there was a Temple, a sacred Centre for the Arabs, and the Jews, and for the black men who sought initiation.

For centuries this Sanctuary of Sinai and Horeb had been the mystic Centre of a monotheistic Cult, and at this time the High Priest of Midian was one Jethro, a black-skinned Ethiopian. (As is well known, Moses married Zipporah, one of Jethro's daughters.)

And it was under the ægis of this Jethro, that Moses underwent voluntarily the terrific psychic ordeal ordained for priests of Osiris who had taken human life.

And when he awoke from the cataleptic trance into

which, as a final test, he had been plunged, he felt himself a different man. He, hitherto known as Hosarsiph, now took the name of Moses, which signifies Saved.

And it was probably in the dark silence of the crypt of Jethro's Temple that Moses heard the voice telling him to go to the Mount of God, to Horeb and to Sinai, to the Mount where from time immemorial a place had been consecrated to supernormal visions of God and of other luminous spirits. Only the bravest and only the highest Initiates dared to venture, on that bleak, barren, rocky height, this encounter with unknown forces.

But Moses was brave and he was an Initiate of the highest order; and it was probably here, under these circumstances, that he saw the psychic light within the bush, and heard the voice telling him to lead the children of Israel out of the land of bondage.

It is not necessary here to recount the story of the Exodus, and the methods by which Moses accomplished his great task, nor to give examples of his great psychic powers; the story itself is well known, and the psychic aspects have been dealt with elsewhere.[1] We only desire here to show that the story of Moses is worthy of a place in Christian teaching, not because it is included in the Bible, but that it is included in the Bible because Moses was an historic link in the chain of great Initiates, who from the beginning of man's existence have been commissioned to pass on to the world at large, those revelations of divine truth which only those gifted with special powers are capable of transmitting.

His aim was the organization of a Society, a nucleus of people who should be the guardians of the sacred truths which he brought out from the darkness of the temples into the light of universal history. So successfully did he achieve this aim, that it was, 1,300 years later, from him that One greater even than Moses, lighted the Torch which has illumined the whole world.

Now is it likely that all this could have been accomplished by one who, according to Church teaching, was only a

[1] *Ancient Lights*, pp. 61-110.

MOSES

Hebrew foundling, who when selected by Providence, seemed to have no special qualifications for his task? Can we really believe that the historic and cultural atmosphere into which Moses was born, was adequately represented by that basket of bulrushes? Is it not time that the Churches began to study that science—psychic science—which alone makes the Bible an intelligible book?

PYTHAGORAS

(*approximately* 582 B.C.)

THE genealogical succession of Witnesses to the Divine, was never more clearly illustrated than in the person of Pythagoras.

He lived towards the end of the sixth century B.C. about the same period in which Lao-Tzu was rekindling religious fervour in China, and when the Buddha was preaching on the banks of the Ganges. At this time, in Greece, the influence of the teaching of Orpheus had waned; the moral and spiritual power of the temples was annulled; the priests had become politically corrupt, and even the sacred mysteries were abused.

But the need for Religion and a desire to revive memories of a sacred Past, were already beginning to be felt, and inspired minds were instinctively groping for traditions of the ancient inspiration. In this way, as Mead tells us,[1] interest was gradually reawakening in the archaic fragments of the Orphic poems which enshrined the ancient elements of the religious traditions of Hellas; these were collected and translated into the Greek of the period, and once more the old oracular wisdom was placed within reach, and awaited only the magic intellect of a Pythagoras to rekindle its dying embers, and to re-establish its basic truths in the fickle hearts of men.

It seems undoubted that it was largely upon the ideas contained in the inspirational wisdom of these Orphic fragments, that Pythagoras founded his system of esoteric

[1] *Fragments of a Faith Forgotten*, p. 38.

PYTHAGORAS

philosophy. Mead tells us that those who studied these matters most deeply in later Greece, assert with one voice that the line of their descent was from Orpheus, through Pythagoras and Plato.

To the more purely inspirational, prophetical, and oracular religion of Orpheus, Pythagoras added the intellectual accretions of a more cultured age. Pythagoras was, for the laity of Greece, what Orpheus had been to the priesthood. He translated the religious thought of his predecessor into the intellectual requirements of his day, and by his scientific and his moral teaching he gave practical proof of the value of the Orphic inspirations. But, like all those who deal with the science of the soul, he, even Pythagoras, though he removed some of the outer casings which had enshrouded the sacred mysteries, retained those inner veils which could only be lifted by the elect.

Now those who disbelieve in psychic phenomena, or who regard such phenomena as a form only of black art, are in the habit of decrying the Mystery-Institutions of the Ancients; and even those who write impartially about the Mysteries, use metaphysical language which obscures all meaning, and they studiously refrain from explaining that the Mystery-Institutions were, presumably, holy places set apart for the exercise of metapsychic faculties, employed for the purpose of gaining wisdom by intercourse with those holier spirits who only respond to appeals from the holiest and the noblest.

But the greatest thinkers among the Greeks believed and knew that the Mystery-side of religion was the vestibule to the higher spiritual wisdom; therefore they never failed to praise the Mysteries as conducive to morality and to belief in a future life.

The fact that later the Mystery-Institutions were prostituted for ignoble ends, though it testifies to the weakness of human character, is not a proof of the intrinsic evil of such institutions. The indication of the real nature of the Mysteries is to be seen, not in the political Eleusinia or in other disorderly elements of Oriental Cults, but in the best of the Orphic and of the Pythagorean traditions. Indeed, those who gave themselves entirely to holy living were said to live the Orphic life, and the Orphic communities, for those who craved a religious life, were the precursors of the famous School which, as we shall see, was established at Croton by Pythagoras.

The Pythagoreans—says Mead—who regarded the Mysteries with profound reverence, were famous throughout antiquity for the purity of their lives and the loftiness of their aims. Indeed, the philosophy of Pythagoras was an application of his intellect, especially of his mathematical genius, to the best in these Mystery-traditions. And he himself, one of the chief founders of Greek philosophy, is said to have been initiated into the Egyptian, Chaldean, Orphic, and Eleusinian Mysteries; though the inner experiences of this life were kept a profound secret and were not paraded on the house-tops. Indeed from the story, as told in fascinating manner by Schuré in *Les Grands Initiés*, and from which the following account is derived, we see clearly that with Pythagoras, as with his great predecessors, whom we have already discussed, the psychic element was the foundation of his teaching and of his greatness.

He was the son of a rich jewel-merchant at Samos, and of Parthenis. The latter must have been of a spiritual and psychic bent of mind, for on the honeymoon the young couple consulted the Pythoness at Delphi. She foretold that they would have a son who would be useful to all the world in all times: and she then bade them go to Ledon in Phœnicia, in order that the predestined son should be moulded and born, away from the troublous influences of his country. Thus before his birth Pythagoras was dedicated to the gods or spirits.

This child of Parthenis was beautiful, gentle, and full of a sense of justice. He had from childhood a precocious love of learning, and at an early age he used to confer freely with the priests of Samos and with the learned men.

PYTHAGORAS

But none of them satisfied him. He was always searching, amidst their contradictory teachings, the Unity of the Great Whole. The lascivity, the brutality of the Court of Polycrates—how could all this be reconciled with goodness, truth, and beauty?

And one night, whilst meditating on these things, and gazing into the starry heavens, he had an illumination, in which all the Mystery of the Universe was laid bare. In a flash he saw clearly Truths which were inexpressible in human language.

How then was he to interpret with the intellect, these truths which he had perceived by psychic means? Then he remembered a saying he had heard as a child: The Greeks may possess the science of the gods; it is only in Egypt that can be found the science of God.

Therefore after visiting Africa, Asia, Memphis, and Babylon, and learning all that he could glean from their wise men, he went to Egypt, and there he endured the tests, trials, terrors, and ecstasies of an Initiation which lasted for twenty years. He underwent experiences which made it possible for him to realize, not as theory, but as experienced fact, the doctrine of the Logos, of the Universal God, and of human evolution.

And at every step of the steep ascent, the trials increased in severity. It was necessary even to risk life a hundred times if he wished to reach the stage of being able safely to handle occult forces. But he was undaunted, for his visions had shown him the life beyond.

The Egyptian priests soon recognized in Pythagoras his extraordinary strength of soul and character; they opened for him all the treasures of their experience, and he steeped himself in their lore. From the priests of Memphis he learned that the two magic keys which open all the doors of the universe, are the science of numbers and the art of Will Power. It was in Egypt that he came to understand the principle of the involution of spirit in matter, by universal creation, and of its evolution through the development of consciousness.

Then at the moment when he was on the point of returning to Greece, his initiation completed, Cambyses conquered Egypt, and Pythagoras was taken as a prisoner to Babylon.

This apparent calamity was, however, in effect an advantage for him, as the Persian wise men had a unique practical knowledge of certain occult arts. They specially understood the handling of psychic or astral lights; at their command, lamps lighted themselves and radiant spirits manifested.

The Magi called this incorporeal fire, which they could condense or dissipate at will, " celestial lion," and the electrical currents of the atmosphere, which they were said to be able to aim as an arrow upon men, they called " serpents." Is it not possible that when the writer in Genesis tells the story of the rod of Moses which became a serpent and swallowed up similar serpent-rods of the magicians, he is referring not to live serpents—this is a misinterpretation of the translator—but to the flames of psychic light, astral light, electrical currents of the atmosphere, which were called " serpents of light," and which Moses and the magicians could, like many modern mediums, produce at will.

The Persian Magi had also made a special study of the power of suggestion. For the evocation of spirits they used formulas graduated and borrowed from the most ancient languages; for, said they, these barbarous names of evocation must not be changed, as they are the pantheistic names of God; they are magnetized by the adoration of the multitude, and their power is ineffable.

As we can suppose, after his Egyptian and Chaldean initiations, Pythagoras knew considerably more than any of his Greek teachers, either lay or sacerdotal. The gross veil of matter had been torn from before his eyes.

He is said to have had the gift of healing souls as well as bodies; of talking with animals, and even with rivers; of controlling wild beasts by his words; of being in two places at once—a useful accomplishment; of being able to hear the music and harmony of the spheres; of prophesying. He prophesied accurately the downfall of Greece, the time when the barbarians would destroy the Temple, and when shepherds would feed their flocks on the ruins of Delphi.

He knew, too, that all religions are refractions from the same light, and that of all these he held the key, namely, esoteric science.

Having been imprisoned for twelve years, Pythagoras returned to Samos after an absence of thirty-four years. He found his country crushed, the schools and temples shut; the wise men and the poets had fled before the Persians.

But he had the joy of finding still living his mother Parthenis, who alone had believed he was not dead, but that he would return to accomplish his high mission in accordance with prophecy.

And then together, mother and son fled with their possessions into exile, to Greece, he to begin his great work—to re-awaken the sleeping gods in the sanctuaries. He went from city to city instructing the priests in the wisdom he had learned in Egypt and in Babylon, and from the wise men of Chaldea. And then he went to Delphi.

Now the arts of clairvoyance and of divination were well understood in Greece, and in the temple of Delphi they were practised by women, young and old, who were called Pythonesses. Indeed, divination had up to a certain date been cultivated with a religious and scientific sincerity which had raised it to the level of a sacred cult. On the frontal of the temple was the inscription " Know Thyself." And above the door of entrance was inscribed " Only those who have pure hearts may enter here."

But when, having made the tour of the other Grecian temples, Pythagoras came to Delphi, he found that the art of divination was declining, and it was necessary for him to rekindle and purify the flame.

And at that moment, fortunately, indeed, he found at Delphi a marvellous instrument for his purpose, which seemed to have been specially provided by Providence. Théocléa, a young girl in the college of priestesses, was of a highly refined and spiritual nature. Clairvoyant and clairaudient herself, she realized that the priests of Apollo, with whom she had to associate, had not the illumination and the true light which she sought. And when she first heard the voice of Pythagoras echoing truth as it resounded from the columns of the Sanctuary, she knew at once that she was in the presence of the Master whom she sought. And Pythagoras, with clairvoyant prescience, also knew that here was one who would be able in purity and in truth, to interpret his ideas and infuse into the temple a new spirit. At once they both knew that each was the spiritual counterpart of the other.

And this is how Théocléa was made Pythoness of the Temple. One day, says Schuré, she had fallen into a deep trance. Five prophets surrounded her, but she remained insensible to their voices and their touch. Then Pythagoras approached and said: "Arise and go where my thoughts send you; for now you are the Pythoness."

At the voice of the Master a shudder shook her; she rose, her whole body in vibration. Her eyes were shut and she saw clairvoyantly.

" Where art thou ? " asked Pythagoras.

" I ascend. I keep on ascending."

" And now ? "

" I float in the light of Orpheus."

" What do you see in the future ? "

" Great wars . . . men of brass . . . white victories. Apollo comes back to inhabit his sanctuary, and I shall be his voice. But thou—his messenger—Alas! Alas! Thou wilt leave us. . . . And thou wilt carry the light to Italy."

The clairvoyant girl, with closed eyes, spoke for a time in her musical, halting, rhythmical voice; then of a sudden, with a sob, she fell as dead.

PYTHAGORAS

And so Pythagoras, having poured into the soul of Théocléa the purest teaching, made of her a fitting instrument for divine messages. And this practical exemplification of the truths which he taught, filled the priests with admiration, aroused their enthusiasm, and reanimated their faith. The Temple had now indeed an inspired Pythoness, and priests who were initiated in the divine arts and sciences. Delphi became once more a Centre of religious life and action.

Pythagoras remained there for one year, and it was only after he had instructed the priests in all the secrets of his doctrine, and had moulded Théocléa for his ministry, that he left Delphi.

His next step is of special interest. At Croton he founded a College for the initiation of the laity. Briefly, its aim was to make religion scientific and science religious. From a study of moral duties, and a study of the physical universe, Pythagoras led up to the secret of secrets, the study of the soul. Know yourself and you will know the universe of the gods, the secret of the wise Initiates.

It is interesting to notice that Pythagoras took special pains to educate women for the important rôle which, owing to their greater psychic powers, they inevitably played in the religious rites of antiquity. He gave them not only a science of practical domestic and married life—from which some of us might benefit to-day—but instruction in all branches of physics, politics, science, and philosophy.

To make the truths learnt in the sacred Mysteries shine through the earthly life of his disciples, both male and female, this was the ideal at which Pythagoras aimed.

There were four degrees of Initiation, and of these the fourth was the most difficult, as it consisted in putting into practice in everyday life, the truths which had been learnt intellectually and spiritually. But only when Man had acquired knowledge, and the power of will to lead a life of purity and abnegation, could he become a true adept, with occult powers at his command.

The final instructions were given at night, on the shores of the sea, or on the terraces of the temple of Ceres, or in the crypts of the Sanctuary, where the Egyptian naphtha lamps spread a soft and even light.

Women Initiates assisted at these nocturnal reunions, and sometimes priests and priestesses from Delphi and from Eleusis came to confirm the teaching of the Master, by giving practical demonstrations of psychic phenomena, such as clairvoyance, etc., or by relating some of their own psychic experiences.

And then at the age of sixty, Pythagoras performed the crowning act of abnegation. He married. He had two sons and two daughters, who were all worthy of their upbringing.

He lived for thirty years at Croton, exercising an extraordinary influence, not only spiritually, but politically, and for a quarter of a century his power was supreme.

Porphyry relates that 2,000 citizens of Croton gave up their customary lives and joined together to live, with their wives and children, a community life.

But when he had reached the age of ninety years, the reaction against his authority began. An individual named Cylo, who had long nourished hatred against Pythagoras, because the latter had rejected him as a disciple, stirred up the people against him and set fire to the house in which Pythagoras and forty of his noblest disciples were assembled. With two exceptions they all perished.

But the Truth he taught was immortal, and its essence was preserved not only in the hearts of the faithful, but in the *Vers dorés* of Lysis, in the commentaries of Hierocles, in the fragments of Philolaus and of Archytas, as well as in the *Timæus* of Plato, which contains the Pythagorean cosmogony ; and in many of the ancient writers, who are full of praise of the philosophy of Croton. The neo-Platonists of Alexandria, the Gnostics, and even the early Fathers of the Church, cite him as an authority, and realize that he presents a reasoned reproduction of the esoteric doctrines of India and of Egypt.

The order of the Pythagoreans, although dispersed, lasted for 250 years, and his teaching lives on to-day, because the Torch of Truth which he upheld was handed on, as we shall see, to Plato, and to those who followed after.

THE BUDDHA
(622–543 B.C.)

THE story of the Buddha as recorded by some of his biographers presents the greatest miracle in history. For these biographers admit that he was the founder of a religion which numbers even to-day, twenty-five centuries after his death, about 250 million souls, approximately one-third of the human race, yet they assert (*a*) that the founder of this religion had nothing more cheerful to offer to his spiritually hungry millions than the depressing and pernicious doctrine of Annihilation ; (*b*) that all accounts of the Buddha's supernormal faculties must be disregarded as nonsense. The first of these assertions, however, is belied by the moral benefits and spiritual happiness that have resulted to a large portion of mankind from the principle enunciated by the Buddha : and the second assertion can be ignored, because if we deny to the Buddha the possession of any supernormal faculties, and if he was thus unprovided with signs and wonders whereby to attract attention, we are assigning to his teaching, which is said to be depressing and pernicious and humanly distasteful, the more miraculous properties. We shall, therefore, here present what seems to be a common-sense account drawn from various sources, of the main features of the life of this great Prophet.

The word Buddha is not a proper name. It means —from Budh, to know—the Learned, the Enlightened, or the Intelligent One. The Buddha's family name was Gautama, and his individual name was Saddhartha. He

THE BUDDHA

was born about the middle of the fifth century B.C., of royal parentage, in Central India. He was therefore contemporary with Pythagoras and with Lao-Tzu. Thus in three widely different portions of the globe the lamplighters of God were lighting simultaneously their inextinguishable lamps.

Before his birth, the Brahmans had predicted that he would become a holy man and would wander in beggary and want. His parents therefore took every precaution to prevent the fulfilment of this prophecy. They married him to a beautiful and charming princess and surrounded him with every luxury. But all in vain. The young Prince was always meditating how he could redeem mankind from ignorance and from the suffering that comes from ignorance.

And then, of course, as in the other stories we have sketched, he was granted visions—three successive visions—of angels, who appeared under the guise respectively of old age, of disease, and of death. These caused him to meditate still more earnestly on how he could reduce the suffering of the world. And then when the appropriate moment had arrived, another vision was vouchsafed—doubtless by means of the practice of Yoga. A spirit appeared and told him that the time had now come for him to reveal himself to the world. He was now to set forth upon his mission.

From that moment all the attempts, desperate attempts of his relations to keep him from his purpose were unavailing, and one night he evaded the guards set by the King to prevent his departure, took a last long look at his young wife sleeping with her hand upon the head of their new-born babe, the much-prized heir to the kingdom, and with only his favourite charioteer (by name Chondaka) he escaped from the thraldom of domestic happiness and of princely luxury.

And so, at the age of twenty-nine years this young Prince, world-renowned for his beauty of person, as well as for his wisdom, inspired from the spirit-world, abandoned wife, child, palaces, and earthly pleasure, and set forth to seek and to help others to find the secret of the Universe.

He first learned all that the Brahmans could teach him, but he remained unsatisfied. He then underwent years of rigorous self-mortification and asceticism. It was during this time that Mara, the great Tempter and evil spirit, appeared to him and urged him to desist from his mission, and promised him—always the same old story—all the kingdoms of the world and the glory of them, if he would give up his enterprise.

He, however, continued his visions and his ecstasies, until at last one day, whilst seated in semi-trance, under the shade of a large fig-tree, subsequently called the Tree of Wisdom, he had a glorious and convincing vision. The Archangel Brahma came and ministered to him, and he attained what he knew to be perfect wisdom.

This wisdom closely resembled in its main features the wisdom of Jesus, in that he preached Love and Universal Charity as the key to spiritual wisdom, freedom, and enlightenment, and in that he did not advocate a torturing self-mortification. The mind must be purified from sensuousness, evil passions, and unholy desires, but these moral evils would not be eliminated by torturing the body. The great essential was the change of heart.

Like all Great Ones he was diffident of his powers, but he finally overcame his scruples by the argument that one-third of mankind is in error and will remain in error; one-third has the truth and will keep it; but that one-third is uncertain—and these he might save. Therefore, with overwhelming pity for the number of beings plunged in uncertainty, he determined to overcome his diffidence, and he fixed the basis of his doctrine, with the intention of opening for mankind " the gates of immortality."

And here we must refer briefly to the doctrine generally misunderstood, the doctrine of Nirvana. When he promises to the faithful cessation of existences after this life, he means cessation from the dreary round of earthly reincarnations, in which, as he believed, man is otherwise involved. He does not mean annihilation, as is so often supposed. How could he, as he does, talk of immortality if he had annihilation in his mind ?

For instance, when he started on his mission, after that night under the tree of wisdom, an acquaintance struck with his appearance, asked him what religion it was that made him so glad, and yet so calm, and where he was going, and Gautama replied, " I am now going to the city of Benares, to establish the kingdom of righteousness, to give light to those enshrouded in darkness and to open the gate of immortality to men."

Again we are told that as his last hour approached, the Buddha summoned his disciples, and after a moment's silent meditation he addressed himself to Ananda—his relative as well as his favourite disciple, thus : " When I shall have disappeared from the state of existence and be no longer with you, do not believe that the Buddha has left you, and ceased to dwell among you. Do not think, therefore, nor believe, that the Buddha has disappeared and is no more with you."

It is besides clearly stated that Gautama told his disciples that he had already entered Nirvana while yet in the body. And in alluding to a sage still in the flesh, the Buddha is reported to have said, " He is indeed blest, having conquered all the passions, and attained the state of Nirvana." " Many," he said, " have reached Nirvana even in this life." Clearly, therefore, reaching Nirvana meant for the Buddha what gaining the Kingdom of Heaven meant to the Christ.

Again, is it likely that his doctrines would to-day be held by the larger portion of the human race, if all that he was holding out to them was annihilation ? Is it not the ignorance, malice, and jealousy of other religious teachers which have caused Buddhism to be maligned in this respect ? Sacerdotalism is never likely to approve of a Creed which offers salvation without the aid of sacrifices or the assistance of priests. Hence, possibly, an explanation of the otherwise inexplicable opposition of the Churches to spiritualism.

Again, in the latest summary of the essential doctrines of what is known as " The Great Vehicle " it is laid down that, " Nirvana is not the annihilation of the world and the putting an end to life ; but it is to live in the whirlpool of birth and death and yet be above it." And we must remember that as with Pythagoras, Lao-Tzu, and Jesus, the Buddha taught by word of mouth, that is, spiritually, by inspiration. And then it was not he who spoke but a divine " Presence," which " quickened " his hearers of all tongues to understand the one language of universal Love and compassion ; and thus he spoke to every man in his own tongue. He himself gives an illustration of this : " When I used to enter into an assembly . . . before I seated myself there . . . I used to become in colour like unto their colour and in voice like unto their voice. . . . But they knew me not when I spoke, and would say, ' Who may this be who thus speaks ? A man or a god ? ' Then, having instructed them . . . I would vanish away." An experience of inspirational speaking, a glorified form of trance-speaking which is well understood by spiritualists to-day.

He left no writings, and from the travesty of the Christianity of Jesus which has resulted from the various Councils of the Christian Churches, can we not suppose that the Councils which after the Buddha's death solemnly sat to fix the doctrines that were to be considered as binding and orthodox—composed, as they must have been, if we take an average of ordinary mankind, of a few great minds, but of many mediocre and inferior—can we not suppose that these Councils grievously travestied the esoteric, wise, and inspired teachings of their great Master ?

Many of his biographers and most ecclesiastics profess to be shocked at the Buddha's omission of any teaching concerning God. But in comparison with some of the current anthropological absurdities of the Divine Being whom we have surnamed God, the Buddha's silence is a token of reverence which we might well imitate.

What, however, can be said about the astonishing miracles

THE BUDDHA

which are attributed to Gautama? Now in many of the stories which have come down to us concerning his psychic marvels, there is doubtless much that is purely legendary and much that is incredible and fictitious, but surely it is as foolish to reject all the episodes of supernormal happenings in the history of the Buddha, as it is to reject them all or to accept them all in the life of the Christ, or of any of the other great Teachers whom we have named. " By their fruits shall ye know them." And it is only by a knowledge of present-day possibilities in psychic happenings that we can judge as to the plausibility of this, that, or the other phenomenon recorded.

Those of us, for instance, who have been privileged to see what are called " apports " of flowers descend in broad daylight in the open air, under circumstances precluding possibility of fraud, can readily believe that the story of the " shower of divine flowers " may have had a foundation in fact, and though in this story as in others, fact may have been augmented to some extent by fiction, we contend that—assuming as throughout we do assume—the reality, under certain conditions, of psychic phenomena, there must have been a substratum of supernormal happenings, of signs and of wonders, to have given notoriety to a teaching which had not within itself the elements of popularity.

And in studying the tenets of Buddhism, it certainly seems to us that from the Buddha and from his religion, as from Pythagoras, and from their great predecessors, we twentieth-century Westerners have much to learn. Our attempts at psycho-analysis, for instance, seem pitiable indeed when compared with the system of psychology of the Buddhists.

And it is interesting to note that for the Buddha the higher powers of the mind were the spiritual, whilst the lower were said to be the intellectual and the psychic. These latter included clairvoyance, called telepathy of sight : clairaudience, called the power of the celestial ear : thought-reading : insight into past history : psychometry :

remembrance of previous existences, and all the usual mediumistic faculties.

And this view of the inferior value of psychic phenomena as compared with the attainment of higher spiritual wisdom will be endorsed by all serious-minded students of psychic science. These latter, however, maintain that the phenomena above referred to are verifiable as methods of communication between discarnate entities and beings still in the flesh, and that they are not to be regarded merely as tricks of prestidigitation, or as hallucinations. They are not in themselves the ultimate aim, but they must be studied as the groundwork, as the basis, as the nursery end of a great science which has for its goal a knowledge of transcendental truths, of truths which might be acquired by modern man as they were acquired by the great teachers of old—if sought with reverence by those duly qualified to attain supernal wisdom.

So-called psychic phenomena are the result either of fraud or of hallucination, or they are concerned with the greatest truth within the reach of man. Will men never decide between these alternatives ? Shall we never advance beyond the hesitancy of the scribes and Pharisees who when overcome by the arguments of Paul could only murmur " What and if a spirit hath spoken to him ? " (Acts xxiii. 9).

It is true that some of the foremost men of science have to-day passed the " What and if " stage of inquiry, and have boldly answered in favour of the spirit, but others are still hesitating to make the final pronouncement. Professor Thomson, for instance (*Inanimate Nature*) admits that " The climax of intuition is mysticism, and those of us who do not practise it must not brush it hastily aside." And he further tells us that, " One of the objects of the lectures contained in his book is to facilitate reaction worthy of the name of Natural Religion, a reaction leading towards realization of a meaning behind the process." In other words his desire is, if we mistake not, to find justification for the study of religion as a science. But—and here lies his difficulty, which a knowledge of psychic science

THE BUDDHA 75

would remove—science and religion are, he considers, "incommensurables. For science is frankly empirical in method and aim . . . whereas the things of religion are beyond science." But we would with all deference suggest to the Professor that he speaks thus, not having himself given that amount of study to psychic science which he would consider essential for definite pronouncement on any other subject. And we would also suggest to him that the word religion connotes to-day two streams of thought which are flowing in opposite directions. There is the religion of the Churches, which rejects empiricism and substitutes doctrines and dogmas which run counter to natural laws, and which thus conforms to the Professor's estimate of its utterly unscientific character; but there is also the religion of spiritualists, who employ empirical methods to test their belief in the existence of spirit and in the reality of a future life—the main tenets of religion—by making experiments which are conducted under scientific test conditions.

It is true that psychic tests cannot always be carried out with the mechanical regularity upon which scientists in other fields of work can rely, but it must be remembered that in order to prove the truth of a phenomenon, it is not necessary to be continually repeating the same experiment Astronomers are not everlastingly testing the theory that the earth goes round the sun. Once proved it is accepted and utilized as a basis for further discovery. And if science is knowledge proved by experiment, and if religion is revelation, revelation obtained by means of those supernormal but not supernatural faculties which we call psychic, then religion, the religion of spiritualists and of the great initiates, is truly empirical in method and in aim.

This is shown by the existence of colleges, institutes, and laboratories which are devoted to the scientific study of phenomena, which lend themselves not only to experimentation, but also to proof by the impartial test of a photographic lens. Religion is thus personal experience in its most concrete form. Without those personal experiences which were the incentives in the lives of those who founded the religions of the world, we should have had no religions, and we believe that the world is to-day irreligious because in an age when men demand proof, and rightly so, for their beliefs, the Churches refuse to *test* by the light of modern psychic experience those supernormal happenings which amply satisfy those who lived within hearsay of phenomena which were at the time regarded as revelations of a divine character.

But it is to-day possible by means of experiments in modern psychic laboratories to affirm plausibility not only for the supernormal happenings which are traditional in Christendom, but even for many of the so-called miracles which twenty-five centuries ago enabled the Buddha to establish his religion.

LAO-TZU
(604 B.C.)

It is impossible to discuss Lao-Tzu, the great Chinese mystic philosopher, without including both Chuang-Tzu, a celebrated disciple who lived three centuries later than his revered master, and Confucius.

For Chuang-Tzu was to Lao-Tzu what Plato was to Socrates, and what Paul was to Christianity, and it was in a large measure due to his desire to confute the materialism of Confucius, that Chuang-Tzu wrote extolling in his brilliant dialogues the transcendental teaching of Lao-Tzu.

Indeed these three names form a Chinese triangle of which Chuang-Tzu is the apex and Lao-Tzu and Confucius are the two basic points. (He was called Lao-Tzu, which means " Old Boy," because at his birth he had the appearance of an old man with grey hair.) It is more than probable that but for the immortality ensured to Lao-Tzu by the brilliant literary gift of Chuang-Tzu, the precious collections of Lao-Tzu's sayings in the *Tao-Teh-King* would never have passed the Chinese wall, but would have been submerged beneath the flood of Confucianism which was fashionable in China in the fourth century.

Again, curiously enough, it is possible that if Lao-Tzu had never existed we might never have heard of Chuang-Tzu, for the latter was not himself a prophet, and but for the inspiration with which the spiritual philosophy of the ancient sage had fired his poetic imagination, he might have wasted his precious literary talent on subjects which had not in them the breath of immortality.

We will here disregard the doubt which has in some quarters been cast upon the authenticity of the *Tao-Teh-King*, the literary legacy of Lao-Tzu, as for those who have even a glimmering of esoteric knowledge it bears within itself invincible evidence of having been written by one—and a Great One—who knew from personal experience the reality of that Inner Light which illumines every page of this exquisite little bible.

This *Tao-Teh-King* is a résumé of the sayings of Lao-Tzu, a hurriedly compiled summation of the chief tenets of his teaching. It is said to have been extracted from him—at the frontier, as he was leaving China to pass his old age in peace elsewhere—by the keeper of the Pass, who became an ardent disciple, and who fortunately for us felt that it would be a calamity were such inspired teaching not to be perpetuated. For, like Pythagoras, like the Buddha, and like Jesus, Lao-Tzu had taught by word of mouth only and not by writings, well knowing that the difficulty of translating transcendental truths into mundane terms is lessened by direct contact with living people whose subconscious minds are, at the moment of listening, attuned to receive vibrations from the Master-Mind; well knowing also that a printed word used to express an abstract Idea may, when dissociated from an explanatory context supplied by the speaker, convey various meanings any one of which is liable to be appropriated by officious expositors or by prejudiced or incapable translators.

The following is, for instance, an example of how the same phrase can be given two entirely different interpretations by two translators who approach the subject from different angles of thought. Dr. Legge's translation of paragraphs 3 and 4 of chapter 3 of the *Tao-Teh-King*, is as follows: " He constantly tries to keep them without knowledge and without desire, and where there are those who have knowledge, to keep them from presuming to act on it."

Whereas according to Isabella Mears, this reads:

> He always teaches the people
> To know the Inner Life,
> To desire the Inner Life.
>
> He teaches the masters of knowledge
> To cease from activity,
> To act through activity of the Inner Life;
> Then Inner Life will govern all.

A rendering considerably more in keeping with the general trend of teaching of an esoteric philosopher.

But from amongst the hurly-burly of disputations, not only concerning the *Tao-Teh-King*, but as to which of the principles enounced in the writings of Chuang-Tzu should be attributed to Lao-Tzu, there emerges clearly this great fact, that already two centuries before the time of Socrates and Plato, there lived in China, where prevailed an advanced state of civilization, a great prophet and philosopher whose teaching as exposed by Chuang-Tzu is far in advance of any religious thought of to-day.

His biographers express surprise at the " extraordinary similitude " which is shown between many of the ideas expressed by Lao-Tzu and those held by Pythagoras, as well as those contained in the Sanscrit Vedas. But if, as we believe, his wisdom was derived from the same source as that which inspired Pythagoras and those to whom the wisdom contained in the Vedas was revealed, we should only be surprised if there were no similitude.

Then, too, Lao-Tzu was imperial historiographer, or keeper of the royal archives, and he would thus have had easy access to the literature of the Western world, and he probably would have known something of the philosophy of Pythagoras, who was his contemporary; and though he himself contributed much original and inspired thought, it is unreasonable to suppose that a mind of his calibre should have been unaffected by the inspired wisdom of his great predecessors.

Lao-Tzu rejected any set system of teaching, declaring that " Those who knew did not speak, whilst those who spoke didn't know " [1] (chapter lvi). Fortunately, however, he spoke enough for us to glean from the scattered sayings preserved and regarded as genuine, not only in the *Tao-Teh-King*, but in early Chinese literature, that he taught the same old Truths that have been revealed by his great predecessors and by his great successors in all time, namely : the Imminence of the Eternal Principle in all that is : that the soul is an emanation from the Divine, and that life is perfect in proportion as it becomes one with that from which it came and loses what is individual in it. The true sage takes his refuge in God, and learns that there is no distinction between subject and object. " This is the very axis of Tao " ; that we must use the light that is within us to revert to our natural clearness of sight ; the relativity of all human perceptions and—2,500 years before Einstein—the relativity even of space and time.

He also taught that we must return good for evil [2] : that the greatest conquest is that of Self : that he who is strong must become weak : that he who would be first must be last : that the goodness of doing good is not real good : also that we may look forward to another and a higher life. He taught that the perfect man is a spiritual being, and speaking generally, it is certain that students of psychic philosophy will have no difficulty in recognizing in Chuang-Tzu's exposition of the teaching of Lao-Tzu, as well as in the *Tao-Teh-King* itself, undoubted evidence that Lao-Tzu was an Initiate of the first order, and that his teaching was all based upon wisdom derived from a spiritual source.

He differentiates the " human intellect from the Intelligence that is of God," asserting that " man's intellect, however keen, can never reach the root." He distinguishes mind, soul, and spirit in a manner which is unintelligible to those who are unacquainted with psychic truths, and apart from the many examples of language which is meaningless

[1] *Tao-Teh-King*, by Lao-Tzu, chap. lvi (transl. by Isabella Mears).
[2] Confucius taught the negative aspect of this sentiment, namely, " What you do not want done to yourself do not do to others."

except to students of transcendental wisdom, he talks of the immortality and divinity of the soul in a manner and with a confidence born only of personal experience of the soul's power of functioning on the spirit plane. "The soul," he said, "is immortal and divine; life and death are all-powerful, but they cannot affect it; to know this constitutes the sage. I will lead you," he says, "through the portals of Eternity into the domain of Infinity. My light is the light of sun and moon. My life is the life of heaven and earth. I know not who comes and who goes. Men may all die, but I endure for ever."

But that which is of chief interest to us in this place is that he professed to have found the clue to all things human and divine, and this clue was—the Tao. What then was this Tao ? What indeed was the Logos of Heraclitus, the Knowledge of Socrates, the Nous of Plato, the Inward Light of George Fox, the Faith which could move mountains of the Christians ?

Here is Lao-Tzu's answer: The name of Inner Life is Everlasting Tao (chapter xxxii, *Tao-Teh-King*). The Tao was, as Chuang-Tzu expresses it, "the argument without words, the Alpha and Omega of all things in heaven and earth: that which could be attained but not seen: which was before heaven and earth were: which has existed for all time. Spiritual beings draw their inspiration therefrom. Once attain to Tao and there is nothing which you cannot accomplish. Without it nothing can be accomplished. That which could only be attained by Inaction. As the Vital Principle said to the spirit of the Clouds, Rest in inaction, Cast your slough, Spit forth intelligence, Ignore all differences. Become one with the Infinite. Release your mind. Free your soul. Be vacuous. Be nothing."

In discussing this injunction to inaction most commentators wander widely from the simple and intelligible meaning which would be attached to it by psychic students with a knowledge of the mental conditions essential for superterrestial revelations, and they assume that the prophet was advocating inactivity, a *laissez-aller* policy in the world of objective life, not realizing the difference in the mind of Lao-Tzu between Tao and Teh, the Inner and the Outer Life. " Be active, with the activity of Inner Life. Serve with the service of Inner Life. Be fragrant with the fragrance of Inner Life " (chapter lxiii, Mears).

But indeed we shall never understand the true meaning of these terms Tao, Logos, and the like, by reading the comments of the learned biographers who discourse upon these subjects, for to them everything that is supernormal, that is, belonging to experiences with which they are not personally familiar, and which they term supernatural, must be " brushed aside as unworthy of consideration." [1]

Thus grandiosely in one sweep they brush aside all religion, all in short which cannot be seen, heard, felt, touched, or smelt by their own physical senses. They even make philosophy, the philosophy of Eucken and Bergson meaningless, for unless there is some reality behind that which these metaphysicians are trying to express, they are only taking us aloft in captive balloons. And the tantalizing thought here presents itself: If only Bergson and Eucken had dared to speak in concrete terms of their abstractions, what a mine of spiritual wealth might have been at the disposal of a world hungering for spiritual realities.

But translated by the light of the spiritual experiences of all those great Teachers, Saints, and Prophets who have been impelled to their revelations and their messages, Tao, Knowledge, Faith, Inward Light, and the Logos, are only different facts of the same transcendental experience, the experience, namely, that Truth concerning God, concerning Spirit, concerning the After-Life, concerning all things ultramundane, comes, and can only come, by inspiration from the world of spirit, by the Word, the inspired Word, by Inward Light, by Faith, by Knowledge, by the Tao.

[1] Gen. Alexander's *Lao-Tzu, the Great Thinker*.

All set forms of religion, all rituals, all doctrines, which fail to recognize this fact, fail to fulfil their purpose ; and the men of to-day who call themselves ministers of religion, but who have merely been college-trained to their profession of the Church as to any other worldly profession, and who have not themselves had that personal spiritual experience which is subsumed in attainment of the Tao, etc., these ministers of religion are in a pitiable position ; they are holding bridal banquets without the bride and drinking to her health from empty goblets, and they wonder why the guests are not enthused. From their pulpits they are striking matches without heads, and they wonder why the sacred fires remain unlit.

It matters little how much either in the *Tao-Teh-King*, or in the fascinating writings of Chuang-Tzu can truly be attributed to Lao-Tzu. The general tenour of his teaching can be clearly deduced, as can that of Jesus, from an instinctive appraisement of the preserved sayings—sayings which must have burnt themselves indelibly into the minds of those who heard them, and passed on to us their spiritual purpose.

The idea of the Tao alone brings Lao-Tzu into line with all the other torchbearers in our series, and enables us clearly to visualize this old Chinese Mystic as one who drew his wisdom at first hand from the true fountain-head. For spiritualists that one word Tao summarizes the wisdom thus derived, and by means of that one word alone we can appreciate the symbolic value for all time of the meeting which took place between Lao-Tzu and Confucius : the one a representative of religious spirituality, the other of mundane morality and ecclesiastical etiquette—an encounter which would be paralleled by a ·meeting between St. Paul and a modern bishop.

For Confucius, although he acknowledged God and sacrificed to the spirits, and recognized the existence of a spirit-world, was evidently not possessed of the psychic faculty, and had no first-hand experience of these foci of spiritual life. Hence, possibly, the reason why he wisely abstained from teaching his disciples about God or the spirit-world. "The unknowable," he said, "had better remain untouched." "Respect the spirits," said he, "but keep them at a distance." Hence, presumably, his popularity amongst the matter-of-fact Chinese.

He therefore insisted that men had enough to do in attending to the problems of everyday life, and that by fulfilling their duty to their neighbour they would best fulfil their duty to God. For Confucius the whole duty of man could be summed up in the command, "Be charitable and do your duty to your neighbour." And like the Pharisees, and all those whose religion is based on morality, Confucius looked to the cleanliness of the outside of the platter, and insisted that external rights and ceremonies should be scrupulously observed—even to the correct position to be assumed in bed.

The encounter, therefore, between Lao-Tzu and Confucius, between two great minds which were in complete antithesis to each other, was of world-wide significance, for it symbolized the two divergent schools of those who, like Confucius and the modern Churches, confound morality plus ecclesiasticism, with religion, and are content to preach the ten commandments and the observance of church ritual, and those who, like Lao-Tzu, though regarding morality as a mundane necessity of social life and of social evolution, realize that spiritual truths will never be acquired by obedience to moral precepts and ecclesiastical ritual. For Lao-Tzu "form and virtue, charity and duty to one's neighbour" were the accidentals of the spiritual.

Confucius was fifty-one years of age when he made up his mind to journey South to P'ei to see the renowned Lao-Tzu and to ask about the Tao, and according to Chuang-Tzu the following seems to have been the gist of that great interview: "So you have come, Sir, have you," said Lao-Tzu. "I hear you are considered a wise man up North. Have you got Tao?"

"Not yet," answered Confucius.

"In what direction," asked Lao-Tzu, "have you sought for it?"

"I sought it for five years," replied Confucius, "in the science of numbers, but did not succeed."

"And then? . . ." continued Lao-Tzu.

"Then," said Confucius, "I spent twelve years seeking for it in the doctrine of the Yiu and Yang, also without success."

"Just so," rejoined Lao-Tzu. "Could Tao be imparted or given, there is no man but would impart it to his brother or give it to his child. But this is impossible . . . unless there is a suitable endowment within, Tao will not abide. . . . You are incapable of giving Tao an asylum in the bottom of your heart. The perfect men of old took their road through charity, stopping a night with duty to their neighbour, on their way to ramble in transcendental space. . . . Being under no obligation to others, they did not put anyone under obligation to themselves. The ancients called this the outward visible sign of an inward and spiritual grace." (If the date of Lao-Tzu had been subsequent to that of Christ, would the world not say at once that he had plagiarized this phrase from Christianity?)

Confucius then suggested that for him charity and duty to one's neighbour comprised the whole duty of Man. To this the irascible old Sage replied impatiently, "The chaff from winnowing will blind a man's eyes so that he cannot tell the points of the compass. . . . And just in the same way this talk of charity and duty to your neighbour drives me nearly crazy. It's like searching for a fugitive with a big drum. Charity and duty to neighbour are caravanserais established by wise rulers of old: you may stop there one night, but not for long, or you will incur reproach."

Lao-Tzu then rebuked his visitor roundly for his ostentatious way of travelling, and for his love of princes, of publicity, and of popularity. "Put away, Sir," he said, "your haughty airs and many desires, your flashy manner and extravagant will; these are all unprofitable to you. This is all I have to say to you."

Confucius does not seem to have taken offence, and so much else that was to him of an astonishing nature was revealed by Lao-Tzu, of ideas utterly at variance with his own utilitarian outlook, and utterly beyond his own mental horizon, of things spiritual and of things divine, on the nature and attributes of the First Cause, and man's relationship to God, that Confucius was completely overcome, tortured no doubt by the thought: Had he all these years been preaching a vain doctrine? that on his return home he did not speak for three days and he did not leave his house for three months. When asked by a disciple in what direction he had at the interview admonished Lao-Tzu, Confucius replied, "At his voice my mouth was agape; I could not shut it; my tongue protruded and my soul was plunged in trouble." He seems to have fallen completely under the spell of the Master mind.

However, at the end of three months Confucius went again to Lao-Tzu and said, " I have attained. . . . Birds lay eggs. . . . Insects undergo metamorphosis. . . . For a long time I have not been enlightened. And he who is not enlightened himself, how should he enlighten others ? "

To which Lao-Tzu replied, " You have attained."

But Confucius seems to have continued his visits, for Chuang-Tzu tells us that on another occasion Confucius went to see Lao-Tzu. The latter had just washed his head, and his hair was hanging down his back to dry. He must have been in trance for " he looked like a lifeless body," so Confucius waited awhile, but at length approached and said, " Do my eyes deceive me or is this really so ? " Your frame, sir, seems like dry wood, as if it had been left without that which informs it with the life of man."

Lao-Tzu replied that he was wandering in the unborn, and he then proceeds to tell Confucius what is, he says, " probably the truth " concerning the First Cause, Light and Darkness, Life and Death, etc. And when Confucius asks him what is to be got by thus wandering, Lao-Tzu answers: "The result is perfect goodness and perfect happiness. And he who has these is a perfect man.... Those who practise Tao understand the secret of this."

Confucius confessed that the virtue of Lao-Tzu equalled that of Heaven and Earth, and he went forth and said to other wise men, "In point of Tao, I am but as an animalcule in vinegar. Had not the Master opened my eyes, I should not have perceived the greatness of the Universe." And one is left wondering whether the materialistic tendency of the teaching of Confucius might not have been modified had he encountered Lao-Tzu earlier in his career. For, indeed, according to what Chuang-Tzu said to Hui-Tzu, "When Confucius reached his sixtieth year he changed his opinions. What he had previously regarded as right he ultimately came to regard as wrong."

But had Confucius not given his utilitarian, his politico-moral and materialistic philosophy to the world, we might have been deprived of the fascinating literary outpourings of Chuang-Tzu, for although the latter was not himself a prophet, he made it his life's endeavour to confute the deadly Pharisaism, the materialism of the then fashionable Confucianism, and it was for this purpose that he used the spiritual philosophy of Lao-Tzu which had so deeply impressed his poetic imagination.

And the world could ill have spared the masterpiece which Chuang-Tzu bequeathed. His work is a succession of Platonic dialogues on philosophic subjects discussed in the form of allegory, fable, anecdote, legend, all full of humour, and the thread which unifies the whole is Chuang-Tzu's exposition of the esoteric teaching of Lao-Tzu.

Who would not study philosophy if Chuang-Tzu's method of teaching it were common? Here, for instance, is an example of how Chuang-Tzu teaches the meaning of "the Identity of all things"; a wise man called Tyu Chi, whilst sitting at a table, looked up to heaven, sighed, and became absent as though soul and body had parted; he buried himself, as he called it. In modern language, he went into trance. In that condition he thus discoursed with Tyu Yu, a disciple. "In talking about the Identity of all things, he said, and in order to place oneself in subjective relation with externals, without consciousness of their objectivity—this is Tao. But to wear out one's intellect in an obstinate adherence to the individuality of things, not recognizing the fact that all things are One—this is called Three in the morning."

"Three in the morning?" asks Tyu Yu. "What is that?"

"A keeper of monkeys," replied Tyu Chi, "said with regard to their rations of chestnuts, that each monkey was to have three in the morning and four at night. But at this the monkeys were very angry, so the keeper said they might have four in the morning and three at night, with which arrangement they were all well pleased. The actual number of the chestnuts remained the same, but there was an adaptation to the likes and dislikes of those concerned. Such is the principle of putting oneself into subjective relation with externals."

It is unfortunate that so few of us can read the Chinese original for ourselves, for we suspect that much esoteric wisdom has been translated in accordance with the materialistic belief of the various learned expositors, but even as it has come down to us Chuang-Tzu's endeavour to confute the materialistic philosophy of his age was obviously conceived in a noble spirit. Needless to say he did not succeed. But did Heraclitus, did Socrates, did Plato, or did even Jesus succeed?

We contend, however, that now to-day for the first time in the world's history there is a chance that spiritual philosophy may succeed in at least gaining recognition as a practical and scientific hypothesis, even as a dangerous rival—a *proxime accessit*—to the unprofitable doctrines of materialism, because for the first time in the world's history it is becoming clear that intercourse between the world of spirit and the so-called world of matter is susceptible of experimentation by scientific methods. When this fact is better recognized and is more firmly established it will no longer be necessary to make a sharp division between science and religion. Indeed, if religion is, as we maintain, revelation, and if revelation can be obtained by means of the psychic faculty, even though it be not on that high level achieved by the great Prophets of old, and if this faculty and its functions can be subjected, as they already can be, to tests conducted in the laboratories of scientific men, then religion and science have already joined hands— and those whom God hath thus joined together, no man on earth will ever have power to put asunder.

HERACLITUS
(535 B.C.)

WE must refer, though briefly, to Heraclitus because it was his doctrine of the Logos which in a tangible and recognizable manner linked ancient Greek religious thought—which itself was linked as we have seen with ancient Egyptian, Persian, Chaldean, and Aryan thought—with Christianity, through Plato, Philo, St. John, and Justin Martyr. Heraclitus believed that he had a prophetic vocation. This probably accounts for the symbolic and difficult language in which he clothed his message, " The Lord," he said, " whose is the oracle at Delphi, neither utters nor yet conceals his meaning." Even Socrates had some difficulty in understanding him, for Adam[1] tells us that Euripides once lent Socrates a copy of Heraclitus's book, and when he asked him what he thought of it, Socrates replied, " The parts I understand are splendid; and I suppose what I fail to understand were splendid, too; only it would need a Delian diver to fathom it " (Diogenes Laertius, II. i. 22).

Diogenes Laertius says that in his youth Heraclitus professed to know nothing, but declared himself omniscient after he became a man, which seems to indicate that he attained wisdom, like all the other teachers we have named, by means of illumination from the higher plane, by means of revelation which mere worldly research was powerless to bestow. And the main feature of this illumination was expressed in the idea of what he calls the Logos.

What did he mean by the Logos? Here again, after reading the so-called explanations which meander in and

[1] *Religious Teachers of Greece*, by James Adam.

out amongst the pages of learned commentators, only to be lost in arid deserts of metaphysics, we are forced, perhaps arrogantly and importunately, to reiterate our belief that only an intimacy with psychic truths can give us a reliable and a practical understanding of what Heraclitus meant by this supposedly cryptic word, a word which was in those days pregnant with meaning, and which was, as Max Müller years ago suggested, of invaluable service to early Christianity, affording to the Intellectuals a nexus between the old Grecian philosophy upon which they had been nurtured and the Christ. The philosophers could not accept the explanation of Jesus as the Son of God, but they could welcome Him as the Incarnation of the Inspired Word of the Father.

Now the characteristics of this Logos of Heraclitus, if we may summarize it from Professor Adam's chapter on this philosopher, were: It was to be experienced: it was universal: it was divine: it was eternal: the Logos speaks through man, but is something apart from his own intellect: it is all-knowing: it is the knowledge by which all things are steered through all. The duty of man is to obey this Logos, but most men, says Heraclitus—who had a deep disdain for mankind in general—though they daily converse with the universal, neither see nor hear it, and behave as if they had a private Intelligence of their own, a sort of individual Logos.

"The Logos," says Heraclitus, again, "is always existent, but men fail to understand it both before they have heard it and when they have heard it for the first time."

It is something which reveals itself in other ways as well as through the spoken word.

And now, in view of the fact that all these attributes and characterizations are applicable to what is to-day known as "Inspiration from the spirit world," to inspiration which delivers itself through the spoken word as well as in other ways, can we not legitimately make concrete, and epitomize in two words the conception of this Logos of Heraclitus, reinforced as it is by the same conception variously expressed as the Nous of Anaxagoras, the Knowledge of Socrates, etc." and regard it literally as the " Word," the " inspired Word," which is as spiritualists to-day believe conveyed to man, as Heraclitus well knew, in various ways from the spirit-world, by means of the various faculties of the soul, the various psychic gifts by which mankind is blessed?

Heraclitus begins his book with the sentence, " Having hearkened not unto me, but to the Logos," thereby clearly meaning that it is not to his voice that he bids them give heed, but to the inspired word, that is to the Logos, the divine spirit, which speaks through him: and we are inevitably reminded of the words of Christ, " Not I, but the Father who dwelleth in me." This it was, this Logos, which spoke through Jesus to such effect that to Philo, to St. John, and to the Fathers of the Church, Jesus became the Logos Incarnate, and so in this definite manner it was by means of this common knowledge of the phenomenon of spirit inspiration that the historical continuity of the doctrine of the Logos was insured—from Heraclitus, through Plato, Philo, and the Alexandrine School, to St. John and Justin Martyr.

SOCRATES
(470–399 B.C.)

SOCRATES is an essential link in our chain of Great Initiates as he bridged a gulf between two worlds of religious thought —the pre-historic and the historic, the ancient and the modern—between the religious philosophy of Pythagoras and the intellectual religion of Plato.

It was through the teaching of Socrates that Plato was led to study those ancient esoteric and Pythagorean truths which shine through the Platonic philosophy. Indeed, as Schuré suggests,[1] if it had not been for Socrates, though we might have had Plato as a great dramatic poet, we should not have had Plato the religious philosopher, who linked us in a definite manner with the spiritual teaching of Pythagoras.

Socrates was born near Athens, of poor parents, about the year 470 B.C. His father was a worker in stone, and Socrates himself started life as a sculptor, but he gave up moulding stone into images of men to mould souls into images of God. The world, he said, could do without statues, but it could not do without God.

His mother was a midwife, it was not therefore to riches or to social influence that he owed any aids to his pre-eminence. Nor was it to good looks, for he seems, from all accounts, to have been as ugly as a satyr. Of coarse appearance, thick-set and squat in build, with projecting eyes that seemed to be trying to see round the back of his head, snub nose with wide nostrils, thick lips, straight,

[1] *Les Grands Initiés.*

wiry hair and irregular beard, in his shabby old cloak, and with his great bare feet, he must have been almost a repulsive figure.

Where then lay the secret of his power ? The power which made him the inspiration of Plato, which caused Erasmus in the sixteenth century to call him one of the saints of religion, and which made it possible for men to say of him that " He was not merely a man, he was an historic movement." [1]

It would be quite inadequate to reply that it was his great learning which gave him his influence and his entry to the highest social ranks. We have in the world to-day many learned men and teachers, none of whom is ever likely to become a Socrates. What then was the secret of this influence, for, truth to tell, he must sometimes have been a little boresome, and his suggestion that he looked forward to carrying on his cross-examinations in Heaven must have filled the spirit-hearts of Agamemnon, Odysseus, and Sisyphus, his intended victims, with dismay.

Is it not clear that Socrates had power as a teacher because he believed in his own teaching and that he believed in his own teaching because it came to him at first hand from an authoritative, an unimpeachable source—from the source of all true knowledge—the world of spirit ?

From this point of view it is interesting to notice that when Socrates talks of knowledge he does not mean accumulated facts, he means that which is, as Adam [2] puts it : " The intellectual counterpart of the Christian conception of faith ; inasmuch as knowledge must—so he thought—bare fruit in the life." His attitude towards earthly knowledge, towards science, could, as Adam says, well be expressed in the words of Cowper :

> God never meant that man should scale the Heavens,
> By strides of human wisdom.

---

[1] *Socrates: the Man and his Mission,* by R. Nicol Cross.
[2] *The Religious Teachers of Greece.*

SOCRATES

It was lack, not of scientific knowledge, but of the kind of knowledge which we should define as spiritual experience that was, thought Socrates, responsible for the moral evils of his day, and it was towards the mitigation of this evil that all his teaching was directed. "Know Thyself," the motto over the portico of the Delphic Temple, was the starting-point and the goal for all his famous cross-examinations. Cast your character into the crucible of self-examination, and when you have discarded the dross, take what is left—if any—it has the properties of clay, and with your own will mould it after the pattern, not of temporal but of eternal things—things-in-themselves.

Know yourself and realize how devoid of all true knowledge you are. This indeed had been the inspiration to his own career. For when Chaerephon asked the Oracle at Delphi if there were any wiser than Socrates, and she replied there was none wiser than he, Socrates realized that this meant that he alone was wise because he alone knew how ignorant he was of the only knowledge which could be of service to the soul.

And so Socrates, with that rare combination of rational intellect and psychic faculty which was his distinguishing feature, believed that we must use our reasoning powers up to the limit of their capacity, but that beyond that point, where reason fails, as it does as soon as we try to understand the things of the spirit, we must realize our intellectual limitations and have recourse to oracles and divinations. Unlike our philosophers of the nineteenth century, Socrates placed Religion at the higher and not at the lower end of the intellectual spectrum. The Gods are ready and willing to help where human reason is of no avail. Human reason, therefore, and earthly knowledge were not for Socrates the ultimate court of appeal for man in his perplexities; and it was, in our opinion, his recognition of this fact that differentiated Socrates from other lesser teachers, and which led his distinguished disciple, Plato, to follow up, along the lines of the Pythagorean and Orphic Schools, the esoteric learning, the psychic knowledge which was the backbone of the distinctive teaching of Socrates.

When anyone came seeking for help which no human wisdom could supply, he would, says Xenophon,[1] counsel him to give heed to " divination." He who has the secret of the means whereby the gods give signs to men touching their affairs can never surely find himself bereft of heavenly guidance. " About things which are hidden we ought to inquire of the gods by divination, for the gods grant signs to those to whom they are gracious."

His advice concerning prayer was that we should pray for that which is good without further specification, believing that the gods best know what is good, and he approves the old Lacedæmonian prayer : " Give us, O King Zeus, what is good, whether we pray for it or not : and avert from us the evil, even if we pray for it." A *multum in parvo* prayer which would save those who have to listen to our long-winded supplications much shutting up of ears. His own favourite prayer was, " Give me beauty in the inner soul, and may the outward and the inward man be one. May I judge the wise to be the wealthy and may I have such wealth as only the wise could bear and carry." Is this the prayer of a Pagan ? Yes, of a Pagan steeped in the esoteric wisdom of Pythagoras, Orpheus, Hermes, Krishna, and Rama, and the sooner we return to paganism of that kind the more Christian shall we become.

But what reasons are there for believing that Socrates had that personal experience of the spirit-world which enabled him to speak with such authority ? Now anyone who has ever heard of Socrates will, of course, know of " the voice " which accompanied him and which intervened in all the affairs of his life. He himself thus describes it : " You have often heard me say," he says, " that a sort of divine thing, a spirit agency (daimonion) comes into my experience. Ever since my boyhood, I have had experience of a certain Voice which when it comes to me always forbids

[1] *Memorabilia*, Bk. IV, ch. vii.

me to do something which I am going to do, but which never commands me to do anything; it is this which opposes my following a political career." And according to Plato, the divine sign, the Voice, performed also the useful function of indicating to Socrates, whom he should admit into the circle of his associates, and whom he should refuse. And it was in obedience to the dictates of this voice that he refrained from preparing any set defence when on his trial. "I assure you, Hermogenes," says Socrates, "that each time I have essayed to give my thoughts to the defence which I am to make before the Court, the divinity (the voice) has opposed me." Or again, "Nay, solemnly I tell you, twice already I have essayed to consider my defence, and twice the divinity hinders me."

According to Xenophon, Socrates claimed never to have been deceived by the voice and never to have misled friends by any advice he gave upon the strength of it. "Although I have reported to numbers of friends the counsels of Heaven, I have never at any time been shown to be a deceiver or deceived." [1]

Plutarch even tells the story that the voice once saved Socrates from a scuffle with a herd of pigs by warning him to turn back from a certain road. Without doubt Socrates put implicit faith in his divine sign, as he called it, and rendered it unquestioning obedience.

But clairaudience was not the only psychic faculty possessed by Socrates. In Plato's *Symposium* we are told, for instance, that on one occasion Socrates was on his way to the House of Agathon, who had won the prize for his first tragedy. Aristodemus was with him, but the latter, on arriving at the house, found he was alone. Socrates was not there. Aristodemus, therefore, sent a servant to fetch the great man, but the servant returned, saying that Socrates had retired to the portico of a neighbouring house and that he was just standing there and would not move.

Aristodemus, therefore, to prevent Socrates from being

[1] *Apol. Mem.*

disturbed, excused him to the company by saying, " Leave him alone ; this is a little habit of his : he withdraws and stands absorbed just where he happens to be." Obviously, then, Socrates was in the habit of going into a trance.

Again, Alcibiades tells a story of how on another occasion when Socrates and he were together in the camp before Potidæa, Socrates, although he was attracting the curiosity of the soldiers, remained standing, lost to the outside world, evidently in a trance, from dawn all through the day and the night till sunrise next morning, when he addressed an invocation to the sun and went away.

Plato was presumably a level-headed individual, and he makes it quite clear that Socrates believed with all his soul in the existence of supraphysical forces. And further, Plato sees no need to apologize for the belief of his master in these things. And therein Plato differs from modern writers such as Gompertz, who, when commenting on the mysticism of Socrates, remarks that " It was foreign to the nature of a man who was common-sense incarnate." Gompertz thus assumes that a man who combined reasoning faculties with belief in supraphysical forces must be a human freak. But it is from freaks like Socrates and those other torchbearers whom we have here discussed that man has learned those spiritual truths which alone make life worth living.

Again, in the *Apology* Socrates declares that discussion with others was a duty imposed upon him by the gods, and that he was confirmed in it by oracles, visions, and in every way in which the will of the divine power was ever signified to anyone.

In the *Crito* we read that he had a vision in the night while he lay in prison awaiting the day of death. There came to him a beautiful woman clad in white garments, who called him and said, " O Socrates ! the third day hence, to Phthia shalt thou go."

And in the *Phædo* we are told that whilst in prison he occupied himself in turning some of Æsop's Fables into verse, and that he composed a hymn to Apollo, all because he had been told in vision : " Socrates, cultivate the Muse."

It is indeed quite clear to those who have studied supernormal phenomena that Socrates was a psychic of no inconsiderable power. But this is placed beyond all possibility of doubt if we take the view of Professor Taylor expressed in his interesting book *Varia Socratica,* that Socrates even belonged to the ascetic Order of the Pythagoreans—that he was, indeed, the central figure of an Orphic-Pythagorean community. Professor Taylor shows [1] that the portrait drawn in the Platonic dialogues of the person and of the philosophic individuality of Socrates is in all its main points strictly historical. In other words, " the demonstrably Orphic and Pythagorean peculiarities of Plato's hero, his conception of " philosophia " as an ascetic discipline in the proper meaning of the word, leading through sainthood to the attainment of everlasting life, the stress laid on the " mathematica " as a vehicle of spiritual purification, and the doctrine of the eternal things, the incorporeal and intelligible Ideas as the true objects of knowledge, are no inventions of the idealizing imagination of Plato, but belong in very truth, as their common faith, to the Pythagorean or semi-Pythagorean group whose central figure twice over receives something like formal canonization from the head of the Academy."

In a word, what the genius of Plato has done for his master is not, as is too often thought, to transfigure him, but to understand him.

From both the *Phædo* and from *Gorgias* we learn that Socrates was a convinced believer in the Orphic-Pythagorean doctrine of the soul, according to which this present life in the body is only the prelude to the more real and endless life to come after the separation of the soul and body, and the chief duty of man is to live for this redemption of the soul by means of " philosophy."

Both dialogues exhibit him as closely connected in a sort

[1] *Varia Socratica.*

of society with Pythagorean foreigners. In the *Gorgias*, a special appeal is made to the authority of a " man of Italy," who is a transparent disguise for the Pythagorean refugee Philolaus. In the *Phædo* Socrates is the central figure of a group of like-minded persons : there are Simmias and Cebes, pupils of Philolaus from Thebes, Echecrates, a Pythagorean, from Phlius, etc. And of Simmias and Cebes Xenophon adds that they are two disciples of Philolaus, whom Socrates by his enchantments has attracted from Thebes. In the *Phædo* it is implied that the link between Socrates and these communities was close enough for some members of the school to pay frequent visits to the philosopher throughout his imprisonment.

Again, the companion story of the *Crito* about the large sum of money which Simmias and Cebes brought from Thebes can hardly mean less than that the Thebean Pythagoreans had made a collection on his account, no doubt with the original intention of bribing the accusers to let the prosecution drop. In any case no one will deny that Plato has chosen, especially in the *Phædo*, to represent Socrates as intimately connected with the Pythagorean communities of Northern and Central Greece.

Plato puts the Dialogue of the *Timæus* into the mouth of a Pythagorean philosopher, and like the Pythagoreans this philosopher supposes the mystery of the world to be contained in Number. It would not be surprising, therefore, if, as Professor Taylor suggests, " the real impiety which was the main indictment at the trial of Socrates was nothing other than an intimate connection probably amounting to intercommunion with foreign Pythagoreans." Hence the accusation of importing religious novelties.

Again, in the *Phædo* Socrates talks of the " secret teaching," that is the esoteric system of the Pythagoreans, as to suicide, and in short Socrates was regarded as impious, not as an atheist, but as an adherent of a *religio non licita* ; in fact, as " the first Nonconformist of note in history."

And that he had himself been initiated in the Mysteries

of the Pythagorean cult is the more probable from the inspired words which flow from his lips during his last hour on earth. He is talking to his chosen disciples on the soul and immortality, and he says : " And I fancy that the men who established our Mysteries had a very real meaning : in truth they have been telling us in parables all the time that whosoever cometh to Hades uninitiated and profane will lie in the mire ; while he that has been purified and initiated shall dwell with the gods. For, as they say in the Mysteries, the thyrsus-bearers are many ; but the inspired are few (Many are called but few are chosen). And by these last I believe are meant only the true philosophers. And I, in my life, have striven as hard as I was able, and have left nothing undone that I might become one of them. Whether I have striven in the right way and whether I have succeeded or not, I suppose that I shall learn in a little while, when I reach the other world, if it be the will of God." [1]

Now we know that the Pythagoreans were deeply versed in occult truths, and that intercourse with the spirit-world was an essential feature of their initiation. Is it not therefore reasonable for us to link up Socrates with his great predecessors, whom we have already named and to suggest that he owed his authority, his power, his influence as a teacher, not to mere earthly erudition, but to wisdom derived from the highest source ?

And surely in the end it was his loyalty to the spirit voice that cost him his life. For it was in obedience to this sign that he not only refrained from preparing a set defence when on his trial, but that he refused to consider alternative penalties to that of death. The gods (spirits) believed it was best for him to depart, and he would not question their decision. " I see clearly," says Socrates, " that to die and be released was better for me : and therefore the oracle gave no sign."

And doubtless this lifelong obedience to a super-governmental authority was one of the main causes of his condem-

[1] *Phædo.*

nation by the State. For to Socrates the authority of the voice was supreme over all other commands. And what would happen if every private citizen claimed the right to get his instructions direct from Heaven instead of from the State? Our modern Churches would probably sympathize with the Athenian Senators in thinking that such insubordination must be nipped in the bud. Do not the Churches, indeed, even to-day adopt much the same attitude towards those who claim direct inspiration?

And so Socrates, one of the noblest men that ever breathed, in the words of Xenophon, "the very impersonation of human perfection and happiness," was made to drink the hemlock, which was handed to him by his weeping jailor, as a warning to his fellow citizens to remember that religion is a statutory institution which, like vaccination, must be imposed by means of governmental lymph, *nolens volens* on all alike, and that no rival to earthly authority can ever be tolerated.

And thus one of the greatest intellectual, moral, and religious teachers the world has known, the man who more than any other rationalized religion and brought it within the scope even of those who are not by nature spiritually endowed, was condemned to death on charges—forsooth —of impiety, and of neglecting the gods. One of the great ironies of history, one of the great religious crimes of a world which cannot tolerate in its citizens other-worldliness, but burns and crucifies those who seek to bring Heaven within our reach.

Such, then, are the salient features which can be quickly gleaned from any Life of Socrates, and, as will be readily admitted, the psychic incidents alone would justify our inclusion of this great Teacher in our series. But Socrates is of value to the cause of humanity for a deeper reason, a reason which makes his teaching of special value to us to-day. For Socrates was the first teacher who gave us an intellectual basis for religious thought and a religious basis for intellectual thought. But unless those who study his teaching have an understanding of psychic science and of the religion of the Great Initiates, they will be misled and hopelessly lost in the wordy metaphysics of most of his biographers. These latter, who are in many cases ignorant of and, therefore, incredulous of a plane of life of which they have had no personal experience, whilst recognizing the supernormal character of the genius of Socrates, are, generally speaking, unable to account for this except along the conventional lines of their own physical intellect, and they therefore attempt to explain everything in terms of abstract metaphysics. They devote pages of wearisome logomachy to explaining along non-psychic lines the meaning and origin even of the Voice, the divine sign, the spirit agency, the daimonion. This is variously described and accounted for in lengthy and complicated fashion, as conscience, tact, intuition, *savoir faire*, common sense, subconscious mind, hallucination of the sense of hearing, etc., till in the end we are left wondering not at Socrates' greatness, but that anyone should ever have had intellect enough to understand that he was great.

But these intellectual writers thus miss the keynote of the whole character and life of Socrates. For if the Voice to whose commands he sacrificed his life was nothing but hallucination in one form or another, the whole story of his life falls to pieces, his inspiration as a teacher vanishes, and he is left as a merely clever, eccentric, and rather crazy old bore. Whereas the simple explanation along lines of psychic science as attested in hundreds of modern cases gives a logical, natural, and religious interpretation to his whole life and mission.

The explanation of the Voice according to spiritualistic hypothesis is very simple. Socrates was clairaudient. He had, that is, the faculty of hearing the voice of the spirit who watched over his earthly destiny. Socrates was, in short, possessed of the psychic faculty. As he himself explained, " no mere human impulse would ever have led me to neglect all my own interest."

If Socrates had only been possessed of a great intellect we should probably never have heard of him. A great intellect alone would not have been sufficient inspiration for Plato who had no reason to look up to the purely intellectual attainments of his master. Gompertz, who fails to understand the true source of the power of Socrates, calls the *Apology* one of the most virile books in the whole of literature, but he acknowledges that its virility was due mainly not to the intellectual and artistic qualities of its genius author, but in larger measure to the greatness of soul, to the conscience of Socrates—the Initiate who had, as he himself declared, dedicated his life to the service of God.

And Plato was thus inspired by Socrates because Socrates was an example of that which Professor James must have had in mind when he said: " A combination of superior intellect with transcendental temperament produces the man of genius." That transcendental temperament of Socrates just made all the difference to Plato who himself had an intellect of the first order.

But what after all was the mission of Socrates? These are his own words attributed to him by Plato in the *Apology*: " I do nothing but go to and fro (by the tables of the money-changers, in the market-place, and in the avenues adjoining the gymnasium, or in the shops of cobblers and other artisans endeavouring to persuade you all, both young and old, not to care about the body or riches, but first and foremost about the soul—how to make the soul as good as possible. And I should be guilty," he said, " of a crime, indeed, if . . . through fear of death or anything else whatever, I should desert the post to which I am assigned by the god, for the god ordains . . . that I should follow after wisdom and examine myself and others."

For his belief was that it was only by vigorous self-examination and by contact of mind with mind that we can find Truth, learn to know ourselves, and discover how we ought to live. Like other great teachers he left no written word : he relied on the inflammatory influence of speech and personality.

A great deal has been said upon the subject of Socrates' belief or disbelief in immortality. Apart, however, from the fact that it is unusual to find anyone who believes in the existence of spirits and yet disbelieves in the possibility of survival of his own spirit, there are innumerable proofs of his belief that human consciousness survives bodily death. In the *Phædo* he says, " I am as sure as I can be in such matters that I am going to live with gods (spirits) who are very good masters. And therefore I am not so much grieved at death, I am confident that the dead have some kind of existence."

Again there is conclusive proof of his belief in a future life, when a few minutes later the argument *re* immortality is wound up as follows :

SOCRATES : And what do we call that which does not admit death ?
CEBES : The Immortal.
SOCRATES : And the soul does not admit death ?
CEBES : No.
SOCRATES : Then the soul is immortal ?
CEBES : It is.
SOCRATES : Good. Shall we say that this is proved ? What do you think ?
CEBES : Yes, Socrates, and very sufficiently.

But indeed what other conclusion could we expect from one who was as Crito called him " The wisest and justest and the best man I have ever known,"—a man who was said by Alcibiades to be, " In conversation the conqueror of all mankind." And who, according to Plato, " Never hurt a single soul either by deprivation of good or infliction of evil," and who, according to Xenophon, was " so pious and devoutly religious that he would take no step apart from the will of Heaven ; so just and upright that he never did even a trifling injury to any living soul ; so self-controlled, so temperate, that he never at any time chose the sweeter in place of the better ; so sensible and wise, and prudent, that in distinguishing the better from the worse, he never erred : nor had he need of any helper, but for the knowledge of these matters his judgment was at once infallible and self-sufficing. . . . He seemed to be the very impersonation of human perfection and happiness."

Could such perfection and such infallibility be recorded of any human being who had no inspiration from the world beyond ?

PLATO
(429 B.C.)

SOCRATES is called by Professor Zeller the Sphinx of philosophy. Doubtless because this Professor, together with the majority of modern intellectuals, misses the clue to his whole teaching. Similarly—and may we be forgiven for speaking with apparent disrespect—much of the metaphysical outpourings of learned philosophical professors concerning Plato and his works reads like nonsense because to our thinking these professors lack the key to the whole understanding of the wisdom and of the mind of Plato. Their spiritual eyes are curtained. These learned writers are like the blind men in the fable who, meeting an elephant for the first time, attempted to gauge its nature by feeling it with their walking-sticks; they each affirmed with confidence that the object which they touched was a pillar or a thick rope, or this, that, or the other, according as they contacted this, that, or the other circumscribed area of the elephant, but they none of them guessed that the object with which they were confronted was a living animal: nor did they at all divine the nature of the phenomenon with which they were dealing.

And so with these metaphysical adepts, they all treat the Platonic life and writings from their own purely intellectual angles of thought, and they are blind to the one clue which makes a symmetrical and a living Whole of the writings of the great philosopher—the clue which is, however, supplied by the fact attested by Schuré in *Les Grands Initiés*, namely, that Plato had been initiated into the mysteries of esoteric wisdom and was, like Socrates, a follower of Pythagoras and possessed an intimate knowledge of psychic truths. Had Plato been in the flesh to-day he would have been one of our foremost explorers of psychic science. What a partnership between him and Sir Oliver Lodge!

For to Plato, science and religion were inseparable, inasmuch as he could not conceive that man could desire knowledge except for the attainment of that which he believed could alone be known—the unseen, the eternal, the divine. For of the seen and temporal, there is no knowledge, there can only be opinion.

And this is the story of Plato's life as told by Schuré. He was born about the year 429 B.C., and he was therefore contemporary with Socrates, and, indeed, as already suggested, had it not been for the influence of Socrates at a critical period in his life, when he was at the crossroads of his career, his name would probably have come down to us, not as a philosopher who embodied the esoteric teaching of Pythagoras, but as a great poet and a dramatist.

It was at the age of twenty-seven years, at a moment when Plato was on the point of producing a tragedy he had just composed, that he first came in touch with Socrates, who was, according to his wont, disputing with his disciples in the gardens of the Academy. This interview revolutionized Plato's life, and caused him to divert the main stream of his great intellect from dramatic and poetic to philosophical and religious channels.

This was, indeed, a great and pregnant meeting—like that between Christ and John the Baptist by the waters of Jordan. And it almost seems as if Socrates must have had a forewarning of its importance, for it is related by Diogenes Laertius that on the night before this meeting Socrates dreamed that a young swan rested for a moment on his knees, and then suddenly grew wings and flew aloft, uttering a sweet cry—an excellent illustration of the relationship which was to exist between Plato and his beloved master.

But that rarest and most delectable of all affinities—the intellectual—must at once have been established between the old cross-examining philosopher and the young Intellectual, and a spark from the transcendental mind of Socrates seems to have fired instantaneously the inflammable genius of the young poetic dramatist. And this is how Plato made known to his friends the Renunciation upon which, after his discourse with Socrates, he immediately decided.

He invited all his friends to a great banquet at his house, which was a favourite rendezvous of the rich and elegant youth of Athens. He spread before them a sumptuous feast, and whilst wine was freely flowing and merriment was in full swing, his friends asked him to recite some of the dithyrambs from his great tragedy which was certain, they said, to gain the prize at the competition about to be held.

In response Plato rose and said, smilingly and calmly: "This is the last banquet I shall hold. From to-day I am going to renounce the pleasures of life, to consecrate myself to the wisdom and to follow the teaching of Socrates. I renounce even poetry, as I realize its impotence to express the truth I seek. I shall not compose another verse, and I shall now in your presence burn all those I have already composed."

This he did, then and there, to the horror and consternation of his friends. These so-called friends then all, with two exceptions, left him in disgust, and Plato, serene and happy, went out to find and to talk with Socrates.

It was three years after this that Socrates drank the fatal hemlock, and Schuré suggests that Plato's real Initiation began then when he had seen his friend and teacher during his last hours on earth conversing calmly with his disciples on immortality and the sacred mysteries. At any rate, life in Athens would be unbearable without the beloved master, and Plato having received the great impulsion, then set himself, as all the great predecessors of Socrates had done, to gain wisdom from other lands. He was initiated in the mysteries of Eleusis, he followed the teaching of various philosophers in Asia Minor : thence he went, of course, to Egypt, to get in touch with the learned priests and the psychic sages, and he went through the initiation of Isis. He did not, like Pythagoras, reach the highest stage of adeptship : he stopped short at the third degree, which gives intellectual clarity of vision.

Then, we are told, he went to Italy, to familiarize himself with the Pythagoreans. He bought for an enormous sum a MS. of the Master, and having thus traced the esoteric traditions of Pythagoras to their very fountain-head, he borrowed from this philosopher the main ideas and the framework of his own system of philosophy.

This must have been generally acknowledged, for Aristotle begins his account of Platonism with the remark that, " It was much the same thing as Pythagoreanism."

But Plato dared not lay bare the Mysteries which Pythagoras had hidden, as all mystics hide their revelations, under a three-fold veil ; his dialogues, however, are a reflection, almost, it is said, a plagiarism of the Pythagorean doctrines, disguised in the brilliantly coloured mantle woven by Plato's own genius.

But Plato was above all things practical, and having satisfied himself as to the source and the goal of all wisdom he set to work to spread his knowledge, and following the example of Pythagoras, he founded his famous Academy, which lasted for a century and was prolonged into the great school of Alexandria, and was the model of the universities and schools of philosophy that have since arisen.

And once again we are made to realize that in order to be really modern, even in education, we must re-become ancient. For, as Mr. Adam says, the keynote and spirit of Plato's teaching was to mature and develop the germ of personality rather than to impress it from without. According to Plato, the cramming of uncorrelated facts, the method attributed by him to some of the professional teachers of his day, was the travesty of true education—a travesty from which we are scarcely even beginning to emerge to-day.

Could it be said that we have even yet grasped, or at any rate applied Plato's main thesis that " the ultimate aim of education is to raise the soul out of the temporal and visible into the sphere of that invisible and Eternal Being to which she by right belongs." He throughout implies a continuous growth in knowledge through successive lives, with immortality as the crown and consummation of all knowledge.

But we do not propose to enlarge upon the philosophy of Plato, firstly because we are incompetent to do this adequately, also because there are libraries of books dealing with the subject. It is, however, necessary for our purpose to try and show that the philosophy of Plato linked in a definite manner the esoteric teaching of the past, of which he, through Pythagoras and Orpheus, was the genealogical descendant, with the theology of Philo, St. Augustine, and the Fathers of the early Church—hence with our modern Christianity.

Even a superficial study makes it clear that in the words of Adam, " It is difficult to over-estimate the influence which the dialogue of the *Timæus* exercised on religious thought and speculation during the last century and a half before the birth of Christ and also in the early centuries of the Christian Era. The *Timæus* did more than any other literary masterpiece to facilitate and promote that fusion of Hellenism and Hebraism out of which so much of Christian Theology has sprung."

This is confirmed by Grote, who writes : " It was thus that the Platonic *Timæus* became the medium of transition from the Polytheistic Theology which served as philosophy among the early ages of Greece, to the omnipotent Monotheism to which philosophy became subordinated in the Christian Era."

The influence of Plato's idea of the World-soul as "made in the image of God" and as "the only-begotten of the Father," the relationship being conceived as that of father and son, is clearly traceable in Christian theology.

This World-soul, too, of Plato is closely paralleled by the Logos of Heraclitus, which exercised such influence in the Alexandrine philosophies and was of undoubted service in making acceptable to the world of intellect St. John's idea of Christ as the Word, the Logos proceeding from the Father.

And equally conspicuous is the affinity of thought between Paul, who said "Seek the things that are above; set your minds on things above, not on the things that are on the earth" (Col. iii. 1 and 2), and Plato, whose aim was to lead us from the Seen to the Unseen, from the temporal to the Eternal, and who wrote "that we may set our minds on things immortal and divine."

And thus we see over and over again that Christianity is no isolated religion—a thing-in-itself which dropped from the blue, free from all genealogical antecedents, but that it had its due place in a series of historic revelations of a supernormal, but not supernatural order.

When Jowett says that "The Eternal Truth of which metaphysicians speak have hardly ever lasted more than a generation,"[1] he must have had in mind the "hardly ever" of Gilbert and Sullivan's Captain in H.M.S. *Pinafore*, else, how with consistency can he in his next volume mention as the literary and intellectual descendants of Plato such inspirers of religious thought as Cicero, St. Augustine, Sir Thomas More, Aristotle, Berkeley, Coleridge, Milton, Locke, Rousseau, Jean Paul, Goethe, Dante, Bunyan, and Bacon?

St. Augustine, says Jowett, was profoundly affected by Plato, and found God and His Word everywhere insinuated in his writings.

Vol. ii. p. 25.

And why was it that these geniuses of religio-philosophical thought found inspiration in Plato ? Why was it that the Fathers of the Church did homage to Plato, and why was it that St. Augustine derived, as he is said to have done, two-thirds of his theology from the pagan Plato ? Is it not because those who are themselves Initiates, even in lesser degrees, and who have themselves had experience of divine illumination, be it philosophic or artistic, can recognize under whatever covering disguised, those basic truths obtained by means of esoteric science which permeate all revelation that is revelation from a supernormal source ?

And thus we see again how the Torch of Divine Truth was handed on continuously from Voluspa, Rama, through all the great Teachers with whom we have already dealt, even to St. Augustine—and beyond. Thus we believe that Plato's famous *Theory of Ideas* was no figment of a philosophical and poetical imagination—of mere literary value for the world—but an insight into a spiritual reality which could only have been granted to one who had scaled the difficult heights leading to revelation of transcendental truth—that truth which is the basis of all spiritualistic belief, as it was the basis of the teaching of Orpheus and of Pythagoras, from whom Plato, through Socrates, drew his inspiration.

Plato in his *Theory of Ideas* was expressing in his own poetic, dramatic, and inimitable language, not only the tenets of his spiritual predecessors, but the present-day belief of spiritualists, and he can only be truly understood by those who believe in the reality of the world of spirit. It was Plato's belief in the existence of spirit which gave force to his doctrine that the true, the imperishable realities are the things which are—to the majority—" Unseen."

And because we believe, after perusal of many of the ingenious and learned explanations of metaphysical writers, that the spiritualistic clue alone illumines, unifies, and makes logical the life and philosophy of Plato, we will leave the metaphysical expositions to those who love logomachy, and suggest quite simply and in all humility that Plato, like Christ, like Paul, like Moses, can only be truly understood when we realize that he had witnessed face to face the reality of the Unseen and had derived therefrom his knowledge of the comparative unreality of the Seen—the basis of his great theory of the Ideas.

APOLLONIUS OF TYANA
(A.D. 20)

THE story of the great psychic philosopher of the Greek city of Tyana in Cappadocia is of special interest as he was contemporary with Jesus, but for this very reason he is little known, as the Christians, who soon began to base their claim to the divinity of the Christ upon His supernormal wonders, were unwilling to admit that wonders of a similar nature could be worked by anyone else. And when Philostratus wrote his life of Apollonius, from which our present account is mainly drawn, the publisher only agreed to print the book on condition that a treatise written by Eusebius, Bishop of Cæsarea, denouncing Apollonius as a magician and an impostor, was included under the same cover—in order that, as he phrased it, " the antidote might accompany the poison." So there they are both together, poison and antidote, and we propose now to deal with the poison.

This treatise by Eusebius had in its turn been occasioned by another pamphlet called *The Love of Truth,* in which Hierocles, a provincial governor under the Emperor Diocletian, had drawn a parallel between Apollonius and Jesus, and had tried to show that Apollonius had been as great a sage, as holy a man, and as wonderful in working miracles and in exorcising demons, as Jesus Christ. And in the *Life of Apollonius,* by Philostratus, which is available to-day, together with an English translation by F. C. Conybeare, we find accordingly in quaint juxtaposition, the two opposed points of view, each, in their bias for and against a great psychic, typical of the unbalanced judgments which even to-day men form for and against those endowed with supernormal power.

On the one hand we have Philostratus, carried away by enthusiasm and an imaginative pen, making facts look like fiction, whilst Eusebius, who could not deny the supernormal powers of Apollonius, attributes them, as would the Church to-day, to the agency of devils.

But we are indebted to Julia Domna, the psychical research Empress, who together with her husband, Siptimius Severus, was an ardent student of occult science, for the fascinating book by Philostratus. Beautiful, clever, attractive, and of strong character, Julia Domna, who died in A.D. 217, was the patroness of all the arts and the friend of every man of genius (Gibbon's *Decline and Fall*). She was also a great bibliophile, and she had in her possession, amongst other literary treasures, the MS. of a diary of the Life, Journeyings, and Sayings of Apollonius which had been recorded by Damis, who was to Apollonius what Boswell was to Johnson. From this diary and from other minor sources the Empress requested Philostratus to compose the biography of Apollonius.

It is only to be regretted that devoted as Damis was to his great hero, he seems to have been incapable of understanding the real nature of the psychic and spiritual science of Apollonius. His records, therefore, are robbed of much that would have been of exceptional interest to students of psychical research, as he was never admitted by Apollonius to the inner sanctuary, but was always obliged to remain in the outer courts of the temples. He was evidently conscious of his deficiencies in this respect, for he humbly refers to his diary as, " the crumbs of the feasts of the gods."

Apollonius was born about the year A.D. 20. He belonged to a wealthy and well-connected family, and besides having exceptional abilities and a great psychic faculty, he was possessed of remarkable personal beauty. He could have made a great worldly career for himself had he thus chosen.

But from the age of fourteen years he devoted himself

to trying to discover, amongst the numerous Greek philosophies, some school of thought which would enable him to live up to his ideals. And at the age of sixteen he definitely " soared into the Pythagorean life," adopted, that is, the system of Pythagoras, " being fledged and winged thereto," as Philostratus puts it, as " by some higher power." For Pythagoras had, he said, " taught him to be aware of the gods whether they are seen or not seen."

But Apollonius was not a Pythagorean in theory only, as most of us are Christians in theory only. He put his principles into practice. His food was fruit and vegetables : he abstained from wine, because though it was a clean drink . . . it endangered the mental balance and system, and darkened as with mud the ether which is in the soul. He went barefoot : he let his hair grow long : and declining to wear any animal product, he wore only linen garments.

In order to secure peace and freedom from worldly distractions, he lived at Ægæ in the temple of Æsculapius. The atmosphere must have been laden with psychic influences, as for centuries this temple had been a centre to which men had flocked to consult the gods.

Marvellous cures are attributed to Apollonius, for like his great master, Pythagoras, he considered healing the most important of the divine arts ; and, in addition, under his guidance, the temple became also a centre for philosophy and for the science of religion. His aim was to purify the temple worship and to reform the ancient Greek religion from within, by revising, along Pythagorean lines, the understanding of the spiritual truths which were at the base of the esoteric mysteries.

On coming of age he distributed the fortune he had inherited from his father amongst his relatives, retaining for himself a bare pittance. And thus his favourite prayer was : Oh, ye gods, grant unto me to have little and to want nothing. Then he took, as Pythagoras had done, the vow of silence for five years—he was evidently not a married man—and journeyed from city to city and from temple to temple instructing the priests and the various communities and brotherhoods, and all those who were endeavouring to lead the inner life, and who looked up to Apollonius as a noble teacher of the hidden way.

But before he considered himself possessed of the wisdom essential to a Sage and true Initiate, he followed the example of the great Teachers whom we have already discussed, and he travelled extensively. He wandered on foot over Assyria, Persia, Egypt, and India, conversing with and learning wisdom from the Magi of Persia, the ascetics of Egypt, and above all, from the Brahmans of India.

The account of Apollonius's visit to the "Monastery of the wise men," the goal of his Indian travels, is specially fascinating. These great psychic sages knew by occult means of his projected visit, also the manner of man he was, and they therefore welcomed him and freely admitted him to witness their inner mysteries.

And even Apollonius was made to marvel at their feats of levitation and at their general power of prescience, which were shown not as an exhibition, but as part of the natural course of events.

And these sages not only knew by psychic means the history of Apollonius in his present life, they also were able to discuss with him the events of a previous incarnation, when he had, as he remembered, been a pilot on an Egyptian vessel. And Apollonius found himself on common ground with these Indian sages, for the good reason that they, too, had derived much of their wisdom from the teaching of Pythagoras.

The influence also of Socrates was clearly indicated in an answer given to Apollonius by Iarchus, the leader of the Brotherhood. Apollonius had asked him whether, since he and his brethren knew everything else, they also knew themselves, and Iarchus replied, " We know everything just because we begin by knowing ourselves, for no one of us would be admitted to this philosophy unless he first knew himself."

And that these men's wisdom was beyond the ken of the worldly knowledge of their Age was shown in all their discussions, which ranged over every branch of physical and of sacred science. Philostratus tells us, for example, that one day Apollonius asked the sages of what they thought the cosmos was composed ? Of four elements ? Not four, answered Iarchus, but five. And when Apollonius further asked, how can there be a fifth alongside of water and air and earth and fire ? Iarchus made answer in words which would be of special interest to Sir Oliver Lodge, who has made a profound study of the ether, its functions, and its uses. " There is," said the Indian sage, " the ether, which we must regard as the stuff of which gods (spirits) are made : for just as all mortal creatures inhale the air, so do immortal and divine natures inhale the ether." Is not this the belief cherished to-day by those who consider themselves advanced students of psychic science ? Have we then made any substantial advance upon this suggestion as to the nature of that intangible fourth dimensional element ?

In the minds of these Initiates philosophy was religion and religion was revelation obtained by divination and by other occult means. " My good friend Apollonius," said Iarchus, on an occasion when he was praising Apollonius for his devotion to mystic lore, " those who take pleasure in divination are rendered divine thereby, and contribute to the salvation of mankind."

And the word salvation embraced for Iarchus both spiritual and physical health, for he declared that among the many blessings which the art of divination had conferred upon mankind, the gift of healing was the most important, and to this art of divination he emphatically attributed " the credit of discovering simples which healed the bites of venomous creatures, and in particular of using the virus itself as a cure for many diseases. For I do not think, he added, that men without the forecasts of a prophetic wisdom, would ever have ventured to mingle with medicines that save life, those most deadly of poisons."

It was with difficulty, as we can imagine, that Apollonius, after a four months' sojourn, tore himself away from such sympathetic and instructive intercourse. For, as he expressed it in his farewell letter, "the Wise Men had shared with him their wisdom and had given him power to travel through heaven. He would," he said, "bring these things back to the mind of the Greeks, and if he had not drunk of the cup of Tantalus (from the cup of nectar of the gods) in vain, he would hold converse with his Indian hosts as though they were present."

Thus he conceived it to be his mission to restore to the Greeks something of the ancient wisdom of Pythagoras. And at the conclusion of these travels he was indeed abundantly endowed with occult wisdom which powerfully enforced his own supernormal gifts, and on returning to Greece he was regarded as a divine person.

Philostratus in estimating the psychic attainments of his hero, tells us that he knew all languages without ever having learned them. This probably means that in trance he could, as many mediums can to-day, speak and understand foreign tongues: he also understood, it is said, the language of birds and of animals: he could read the inmost thoughts of men: and he could, of course, heal bodily sickness and exorcise demons.

He is reputed to have raised from the dead a young girl, daughter of one of the Consuls at Rome, who had died in the hour of her marriage. He stopped the funeral procession and, saying to the lamenting bridegroom, " I will stay the tears you are shedding for this maiden," he approached the bier, and making some passes over the body of the girl, whispered in her ear: and at once she awoke from her seeming death and spoke, and returned in health to her father's house.

And who shall say that a recovery could not have been brought about by one possessed of the psychic power of Apollonius ? For according to occult belief, so long as the chord which unites the astral with the physical body has not yet been severed, restoration to life is feasible. And the clairvoyant faculty of Apollonius may well have enabled him to see that, as in the Gospel story, the maiden was not dead but only sleeping, possibly in trance, and from this it was that he awakened her.

His successful predictions were numerous : he predicted the plague at Ephesus, but he did not only foretell it, he was also able to cure the people from its ravages. His reputation as a psychic was indeed so far-famed that Vespasian is said to have come to Egypt (from Rome) specially to have a sitting with him in the Temple, because, said Vespasian, " you have the amplest insight into the will of the gods and I do not wish to trouble the gods against their will."

And on this occasion Apollonius gave his august sitter a fine example of clairvoyance, " O Zeus," said he, " this man who stands before thee is destined to raise afresh unto thee the temple which the hands of malefactors have set on fire." And at that moment the temple in Rome was being destroyed by fire.

Philostratus makes a fascinating story of an account which Apollonius gives of a séance at which the spirit of Achilles had appeared to him. Apollonius, together with Damis and other friends, were voyaging along the coast of Eubœa. The sea was unwontedly smooth, and all the company, except Damis, were contentedly conversing on general subjects. He, however, seemed grumpy and disagreeable. Apollonius saw he had something on his mind, and asked him, since he could not possibly be sea-sick on such a calm sea, what was the matter ? Damis then complained that Apollonius knew how eager they all were to hear about the séance at which the spirit of Achilles had appeared and yet he, Apollonius, kept putting them off with small talk about the scenery through which they were passing. " All right, then," said Apollonius. " If you won't accuse me of bragging, I'll tell you all about it."

And then he told them that he had first invoked Achilles by offering up a prayer such as the Indians use in approaching their heroes : " O Achilles," he said, " most of mankind declare that you are dead. But I cannot agree with them, nor can Pythagoras, my spiritual ancestor. If then, we hold the truth, show to us your own form, . . . and attest your existence."

Thereupon a slight earthquake shook the neighbourhood of the barrow, and Achilles, whom Apollonius at once knew to be Achilles, appeared. Apollonius asked him five questions, and to all of these the spirit-hero replied informatively: then he vanished with a flash of summer lightning—an admirable description of the psychic light which often accompanies materialization at séances.

Many examples of psychic wonders performed by Apollonius are given to us by Philostratus. Perhaps one of the most interesting was his sudden disappearance from the Court of the Emperor Domitian at the conclusion of his trial. He waited till he had been acquitted, in order presumably not to take undue advantage of his power, and then, uttering the words, " My soul you cannot take. You cannot even take my body, for thou shalt not slay me, since I tell thee I am not mortal," he vanished from the Court, much to the dismay of Domitian, who was so disconcerted that he could not carry on the work of the Court.

Apollonius then reappeared in miraculous manner miles away, in the cave at Dicacarchia, where Damis and Demetrius were at that moment anxiously discussing his possible fate at the hands of the Court. At first they thought it was his ghost and they were horrified, but when they realized that it was himself, alive, they asked him how he had accomplished the miracle, and Apollonius replied evasively : ' Imagine what you will, flying goat or wings of wax excepted, so long as you ascribe it to the intervention of a divine escort."

Thereafter, we are told, all Greece flocked to see him and believed him to be divine, but he never made the least parade about the matter of his escape.

Perhaps, however, the most notorious spiritualistic feat of Apollonius was his clairvoyance of the murder of the Emperor Domitian. He, Apollonius, was delivering a lecture at Ephesus, and the whole town was present, when suddenly he dropped his voice, as though he were terrified and had caught glimpses of some horrible thing: then stepping forward three or four paces, he cried, "Smite the tyrant, smite him." He paused, as though to make sure that the deed was accomplished, then he cried, "Take heart, gentlemen, take heart, for the tyrant has been slain this day, even now, as I utter these words." And during those very moments the tyrant Emperor Domitian was being assassinated in Rome, in accordance with the vision of Apollonius.

The passing of Apollonius at the age of about eighty years also was characteristic. As with Moses, and others of the prophets, no one knows of his sepulchre to this day, and it is open to those who understand something of occult possibilities to conjecture that his passing was effected after the manner of the passing of Enoch, Elijah, and other notable psychics, and that like his great Contemporary, his body never knew corruption.

If, as seems possible, he was, like Elijah, translated by occult means, he also followed the precedent of Elijah, who, on some pretext dismissed Elisha that he should not witness the phenomenon of his dissolution, for Apollonius dispatched Damis on some trifling and unnecessary errand immediately before his disappearance: a device which Damis only saw through afterwards, on remembering the sage's oft-repeated counsel, "Live unobserved, and if that cannot be, slip unobserved from life."

One of the stories told about his disappearance was that he was living in Crete, where he became a greater centre of admiration than ever before—the people insisting, in spite of his protests, that he was divine—and that he came late one night to the temple, which was guarded by fierce dogs. These, however, instead of barking at his approach, fawned upon him, whereupon the guards arrested him as a wizard and placed him in bonds.

But about midnight he loosened his bonds and ran to the doors of the temple, which opened wide to receive him. When he had passed through, the doors closed of their own accord, and there was heard by the prison authorities who had followed Apollonius, a chorus of maidens singing from within the temple, "Hasten thou from earth, hasten thou to heaven, hasten!" And he was seen no more.

It is said that even after his death he continued to teach the immortality of the soul, though he discouraged men from meddling in such high subjects. And amongst a band of youths who were passionately addicted to wisdom —a synonym in those days for study of esoteric science— there was one who was sceptical. He complained that for more than nine months he had prayed to Apollonius to reveal to him the truth about the soul, but that Apollonius was apparently so utterly dead that he couldn't or wouldn't respond to his appeal, or give him any reason to believe in immortality.

However, five days after having delivered himself of this outburst, our young sceptic was discussing the same subject with other young men who were studying, when he fell into an uneasy sleep. From this he suddenly jumped up, as though possessed, streaming with perspiration, and cried out, "I believe thee." When the others asked him what was the matter, he said, "Don't you see that Apollonius the Sage is present with us, and is listening to our discussion, and is reciting wondrous verses about the soul?"

"Where is he?" asked the others, "for we cannot see him anywhere, though we would rather do so than possess all the blessings of mankind."

The youth replied, "It would seem that he is come to converse with myself alone, concerning the tenets which I would not believe." And then he repeated for them the inspired argument which the spirit of Apollonius was delivering. And thus we see that sceptics were converted in former centuries in much the same way that they are to-day, namely, by personal experience.

Further historic evidence of the existence of Apollonius and of his supernormal wisdom is supplied by various facts. The Roman Emperor Caracalla, who reigned from A.D. 211 to 216, honoured his memory with a chapel and a monument. The Emperor Alexander Severus, A.D. 225 to 235, placed his statue in his lararium, together with those of Christ, Abraham, and Orpheus. And the Emperor Aurelius is said to have vowed a temple to the sage of Tyana, of whom he had seen a vision. Also the Emperors Vespasian, Titus, and others undoubtedly were in the habit of consulting him. And since they had all the best intellects of the Roman Empire from which to choose, we may further assume, in corroboration of our general argument, that they visited the sage not to see him perform conjuring tricks, but because he was wiser than most men. Indeed, Vespasian, in his last letter to his son Titus, confesses that they were what they were solely owing to the good advice of Apollonius. And he was wiser than most men because he derived his wisdom from the source of all true wisdom—the world of spirit. This was expressed in one word by Apollonius in his answer to the Consul Telesinus, who asked him, " And what is your wisdom ? " " An inspiration," replied the sage.

Again, he was a teacher and reformer of sufficient importance to be held up by the enemies of Jesus as a rival to the Saviour, and much must have been known about his powers and wisdom within the inner circles of the religious communities, which would have been jealously withheld from Damis and from Philostratus, who never penetrated the deeper mysteries.

For though Apollonius was always ready to instruct those who sought for wisdom, he was chiefly concerned in re-consecrating the old centres of religion, instructing the priests in the realities behind the rites and formulas, and in purifying the spiritual truths which were being overlaid by corrupt forms and unmeaning ritual.

There is no evidence to show that Apollonius and Jesus ever met : presumably there was no personal encounter : but it is undoubted that they were both within a few years of each other, exercising supernormal powers of a similarly remarkable nature.

And now, from a purely worldly point of view, and

leaving out of consideration any reasons attributable to the divinity of Christ, how can we account for the fact that whereas the three years' ministry of Jesus initiated a religion which has become world-wide, the life-long and self-sacrificing work of Apollonius has left no material result, and the world at large is unfamiliar even with his name as a great Initiate?

For this many reasons, both major and minor, could be assigned. But pre-eminent over all there stands this fact: that Apollonius was only a reformer, whereas Jesus was a Revolutionary. And there comes a time in the history of all religions when the cycle of usefulness of their outward forms is outrun, and when, if the substance of religion is to be maintained, this can only be achieved by revolutionizing the methods of appeal to suit the requirements of a newer Age.

Now the aim of Apollonius was the reformation of the ancient Greek religions by orthodox means, by reviving along Pythagorean lines the understanding of the spiritual truths enshrined in the old faith, truths which had become buried beneath superstitious rites and formulas. And we can see now that the efforts of Apollonius were bound to end in a cul-de-sac because the Age had outgrown forms of religion which were hierophantic. For good or ill, in religion as in everything else, democracy was raising its assertive head. Jesus, imbued with higher wisdom, and with vision more far-seeing than that of Apollonius, perceived this instinctively, and He boldly dragged religion out from the dark recesses of the temples into the open streets and market-places. Revelation was no longer to be the monopoly of Initiates within the Holy of holies. Christ shared His revelations and His wisdom with the multitude. Publicans, sinners, harlots, thieves, all were beneficiaries under a democratic dispensation which pronounced that God could be found not only by an exclusive priesthood of esoterically trained Initiates, but by the humblest man, woman, or child who laid himself open to spiritual influence. The Kingdom of Heaven is within *you*. Revolutionary words which broadcasted a knowledge of God and of Him Who spoke the message to the ends of the world.

And now, after a lapse of nineteen hundred years is not another revolution needed if the basis of Christianity—the basis of the religion of all the great Initiates—is to be preserved? As in the time of Apollonius, the spiritual truths enshrined in the ancient faith have been lost beneath a débris of superstition, ignorance, and tradition. And, as in the times of Apollonius, the people have lost the art of finding God for themselves, in the belief that by going to church He will be found for them vicariously through the offices of the priests.

But the position is worse than in the days of Apollonius, for to-day even the priests have lost the power of communication with the spirit-world, and over and over again they can now only repeat revelations which were obtained in the first century to meet the social and intellectual requirements of an age which has little in common with the age in which we find ourselves. We want to know to-day what God, what Christ has to say to us who are living in the twentieth century. Is there nothing which could be added to Christ's messages of the first century to help us in our difficult and complicated times?

The more "advanced" party in ecclesiastical circles are busy suggesting various minor reforms mainly concerned with verbal alterations in the prayer-book. But the Church needs to-day what it needed in the days of Apollonius—democratizing. And this can only be achieved by allowing the people to share in revelation, that is by sanctifying, by making holy, the calling of those who have the power to communicate with the loftiest spirits, and by permitting those who, though not themselves psychic, are humble and pure in heart, and who are reverently prepared, to be witnesses of revelation.

We have thus made an object-lesson of Apollonius because it would be waste of intellectual effort to study the lives of the great Teachers of the Past if from the success or failure of their teaching we can derive no lesson, and it seems clear that if Apollonius, with his marvellous psychic faculties, lofty moral and spiritual character, exceptional wisdom, and great social influence, failed to make reform of permanent effect, it is not likely that the lesser personalities in church circles to-day will be any more successful. Not reform, but revolution, along the lines of established and systematized communion of saints above, with saintly men and women on this earth will alone make God once more a reality, and religion a living force.

PLOTINUS

(A.D. 204)

PLOTINUS is both for spiritualists and for the Churches to-day an interesting and instructive figure. For not only was he, as is universally admitted, the noblest representative of Neoplatonism, but this school of religious thought for which he stood was the consummation of the best religious philosophy of the best of the old Initiates, and its aims and ethics were the highest and the purest to which man could aspire.

Two questions therefore suggest themselves : What was the secret of the influence exercised by Plotinus in his own day, and in view of that influence and of the estimation in which his writings have been subsequently held by philosophers and intellectuals, how can we account for the failure of Neoplatonism eventually to make good ? Why did it never establish itself as a church and as a community ? As a matter of fact it was absorbed in Christianity, but why had it no continued independence ?

The answer to the first question is simple ; the teaching of Plotinus concerning the soul, the spirit, and things pertaining to religion—to revelation—was based on his own personal experience of the reality of the supersensual world, and thus his teaching carried with it the weight of unimpeachable authority. Plotinus, in short, was an Initiate and was possessed of considerable psychic power.

He is supposed to have been born in Egypt, but he was so ashamed of having had to be re-born on this earth that he always refused to disclose details of such an ignominious event. From early youth he determined to devote his life to the search for truth, and after receiving a liberal education in Alexandria, he went to Persia and to India, there to get in touch with the occult learning of the Magi and of the Brahmans.

Then, returning to Alexandria, he sought wisdom from one after the other of the renowned teachers of that city which was celebrated for its schools of philosophy. But he sought in vain, until one day, when he was twenty-eight years of age and had given up hope of finding what he needed, he was persuaded to go and hear a certain Ammonius Saccas, and directly Ammonius began to speak, Plotinus exclaimed, " This is the man I was looking for."

Now Ammonius was well versed in occult mysteries, and it was doubtless this aspect of his teaching which appealed to Plotinus and which provided him with that which he had been unable to find elsewhere in Alexandria. He studied with Ammonius for ten years, and it was presumably from Ammonius that Plotinus learnt the value, for purposes of revelation, of that state of superconsciousness which, corresponding to our modern " trance " was then described as ecstasy, and which is a condition of fourth-dimensional consciousness specially favourable for the reception of spiritual truths.

Jules Simon aptly describes this state of ecstasy to which Plotinus was able to attain, as " a state of the soul which transforms it in such a way that it then perceives what was previously hidden." [1]

We to-day use the word trance, but both trance and ecstasy denote the suspension of normal consciousness and the soul's flight to another, to a fourth-dimensional plane.

The writer of the article in the *Encyclopædia Britannica* (page 336, Neoplatonism) in describing the last of the three stages of virtue in the system of Plotinus, remarks that, " The highest stage was only attained through contempla-

---

[1] Jules Simon's *Histoire de l'École d'Alexandre*, p. 553.

tion of the primeval Being, the One; or in other words, through an ecstatic approach to it. Thought cannot attain to this . . . thought is a mere preliminary to communion with God. It is only in a state of perfect passivity and repose that the soul can recognize and touch the primeval Being. Hence, in order to reach this highest experience the soul must pass through a spiritual curriculum . . . the last stage is attained when in the highest tension and concentration, beholding in silence and utter forgetfulness of all things, it is able, as it were, to lose itself. Then it may see God . . . in that moment it enjoys the highest indescribable bliss; it is, as it were, swallowed up of divinity, bathed in the light of eternity." And this beatific vision of the One was, says Porphyry, an experience which Plotinus attained on four occasions during the six years of their intercourse at Rome.

Now all the biographers of Plotinus, however much they may differ as to the value and the signification of his teaching, are unanimous in naming him as one of the greatest of the "mystic philosophers." But this is tantamount to an acknowledgment of his supernormal powers, for though modern philosophers use the word mystic as a metaphysical covering for their ignorance of the psychic facts for which real mysticism stands, Mysticism to the minds of those who practised it, was not concerned with metaphysical speculations of the physical intellect, but with experiences which brought the soul in direct, in living contact, with the supernormal world.

The term "mystic philosopher" is not applicable to a metaphysician like Eucken, who, though he has an intuition that all is not well with the philosophy of materialism, yet lacks that illumination which can only be obtained under conditions to which he has not conformed, with the result that he merely glimpses from afar a light reflected from a plane which is beyond his own orbit of vision. But it is truly applicable to one who, like Plotinus, has found the Tao and has had personal experience of those spiritual truths which must remain as "mysteries" to those who cling to the sole sovereignty of our three-dimensional consciousness.

There is indeed plenty of evidence to show that Plotinus was an Initiate, that he was possessed of the psychic faculty, and that he used this, not merely to obtain news of departed friends, but to get in touch with the Divine. And in this sense Plotinus was indeed a great mystic philosopher, and when he spoke of the demonstrability of an Ideal Universe as an archetype of the phenomenal world with which we are aquainted, and when he tells us of an Order of Beings of ethereal essence, he speaks thus because he has himself been borne into that supersensual, that " Ideal World," and can no more doubt of its existence, or doubt that it is inhabited by beings of a non-corporeal type than we can doubt the existence of the race of Zulus when we travel to their country.

The secret, therefore, of the influence of Plotinus upon his contemporaries and upon their immediate successors is amply explained. He drew the credentials of his teaching from the highest and most authoritative source, and the religiously minded who were in immediate contact with him could understand that his language was not concerned with metaphysical abstractions of subjective Ideals, but that it represented realistic facts with which he had come in personal contact, and they could accept his religion as a revelation.

And since he presented his truths in the form of reasoned philosophy, philosophers of all ages have been able to appreciate his value as an inspiring philosopher of Idealism.

But—and here lies the answer to our question, How can we account for the failure of Neoplatonism to make good ? —Idealism which has not for those who use the word, a background of reality, Idealism which is not based on Realism, may be the basis of a system of intellectual metaphysics, but it can never be the basis of a live religion. Religion is based upon Realism, and its influence ceases the moment it becomes merely an Ideal.

For here we must distinguish between the meaning of

the "Ideal" world of Plotinus or of Plato, and the meaning attached to this word Ideal by modern metaphysicians. The "Ideal" world of Plotinus and of Plato was not a world merely to be desired but never to be attained. To them the Ideal world was the very real world of Spirit, a world to which, under certain conditions, they had access, and to which men to-day, under similar conditions, can also have access.

The whole significance of the religious philosophy of Plato and of Plotinus loses weight to-day because men attach to this word "Ideal" its modern meaning of a goal of perfection which is Utopian, imaginary, and altogether beyond reach. And so, when after his death, the personal testimony of Plotinus to the authenticity of his spirit inspirations were no longer available, the philosophers of subsequent times, themselves ignorant of transcendental truths, misunderstood, wilfully or otherwise the realism of his teaching and translated his objective experiences into a subjective philosophy. They made of it a mummy from which the soul had fled.

The lesson then to be learnt from the history of Plotinus seems to be that unless the transcendental experiences of any outstanding personage who may have commanded the attention and respect of his contemporaries can be corroborated by similar experiences repeated over and over again for each succeeding generation, these experiences in course of time lose their plausibility and come to be regarded merely as superstitions.

And thus arises the mistaken assumption that Religion instead of being the result, as we believe, of the highest wisdom, is born of superstition and of ignorance. Its pursuit is therefore abandoned by the Intellectuals, and the control of religion—then falsely so-called—falls more and more into the hands of those who have merely personal, social, or moral interests in its upkeep, or who—as with most women—still cling to it from intuition, refusing to face the negation which would, as they suppose, result from intellectual examination of its foundations.

Throughout the Ages, the rise and decline in the value of the religious teaching inaugurated by the various founders of religions have followed the same invariable course. First came the religion, that is the revelation to the Initiate: then came philosophy concerning those revelations. But since those who philosophized had not themselves the means of testing or of corroborating the revelations, they intellectualized these and described objective experiences as states of mind that were purely subjective, with the result that Religion is supplanted by metaphysics and Athanasian Creeds.

And it is this service of corroborating the experiences not only of Plotinus, and all his predecessors, and of seers of all ages, but the experiences also of the teachers, saints, and prophets referred to in both Old and New Testaments, that Spiritualism could render to the Churches, if they would but accept the Service.

The Churches refuse to realize that Spiritualism in the hands of serious students is Religion, Philosophy, and Science combined. It is Religion because it is Revelation, and brings a knowledge of God and of an after-life: it is Philosophy—a philosophy of life earthly and of life eternal: and it is Science, as its laws can be classified and its phenomena can be subjected to scientific experimentation.

It is true that until training colleges are available for the training of the psychically gifted, we are obliged at present to make use of imperfect intermediaries of communion with the spirit-world, but let the Churches remember that to reach the Heavens our flying machines must take off from earth, they cannot start from mid-air. We to-day have this great advantage over the contemporaries of Plotinus in that we have opportunities of testing and of corroborating supernormal experiences in scientific laboratories. Proof and corroboration by scientific methods were not available in the third century, and it is because we can to-day test and verify phenomena which purport to put us in touch with another world, with another sphere of consciousness, because, in short, we can superimpose science upon religion, that we are beginning to learn that religion is science since it needs to be and is susceptible of proof, and that it is only by the combination of science and religion that men will ever find a true and satisfying philosophy of life.

MOHAMMED
(A.D. 570–632)

MOHAMMED is an illustration, but an unfortunate illustration of our thesis that the world's great teachers have been of psychic temperament and have derived their inspiration, their confidence, and their mandates from the spirit plane : for though he was a great teacher and obtained his inspirations from the spirit-world, it is doubtful whether—if we take a long view of the social history of mankind—his teaching has not done more harm than good.

For in spite of the fact that much that was beneficial can be placed to the credit of his account, he gave religious sanction, the sanction of the Koran and of his own shocking example, to the principle to which men in all ages have been only too willing to accede—the principle, namely, of the inferiority of woman. And if it be true that a nation's civilization can be gauged by the social status of its women, Mohammed has condemned millions of his fellow-beings to a state of social demoralization from which they could only now be raised by a renunciation of the religion he bequeathed to them.

He was born two months after the death of his father, who was a caravan merchant, at Mecca in Arabia, in the year A.D. 570, at a time when a Leader, both for political and spiritual purposes, was badly needed. For there was then no central government and the tribes fought amongst themselves, or made pacts with each other according to local and individual inclination.

He seems to have inherited his psychic temperament

from his mother, for it is recorded of her that she was so frequently visited by "ghosts" that her friends recommended her, as a safeguard from the attentions of her celestial visitors, to tie pieces of iron on her neck and arms.

At his birth she is said to have seen proceeding from her body a light which illuminated the palaces of Bostra, and it was, says Sprenger, owing to this favourable omen that the child was called Mohammed, which means "Praised."

In accordance with the curious custom of well-to-do people in Mecca, Mohammed's mother sent him as a baby to be brought up by a Bedouin foster-nurse in the desert in order to escape the pestilential climate of the town, and to imbibe the genuine Arabic character and language. But at the age of five years the nurse brought the boy back to his mother and refused to keep him any longer, as he was subject to "nervous attacks," and was, she said, "shaded by a cloud wherever he went," and she feared the influence of evil spirits.

But when he was six years old his mother died, and a year later his grandfather, who had taken him in charge, also died, and Mohammed was then adopted by an uncle, who trained him to the caravan business. But his dreamy temperament unsuited him for practical work, and he was reduced to the much-despised occupation of pasturing sheep, an occupation, however, which favoured the development of his psychic nature, and was no doubt a factor which contributed to the maintenance of that moral purity for which he was as a young man—but only as a young man—conspicuous.

He believed himself to have been during this time twice miraculously preserved from temptation. On the first occasion, he had asked another lad to look after his sheep while he went into Mecca to amuse himself like other youths in the town. But when he reached the outskirts of the city his attention was mercifully diverted by a marriage feast. He stayed to watch this and fell asleep till the morning.

And another night when he was entering the town for the same purpose, he was arrested by hearing strains of heavenly music. He sat down to listen, and again he fell asleep till morning.

But there came a time when his uncle grew straitened in his means and was obliged to tell Mohammed that he must now take a more active part in bringing grist to the family mill. He suggested that a certain rich widow named Khadija was requiring a reliable man to be in charge of her caravan which was taking merchandise to Syria, and Mohammed, he said, might offer her his services. Mohammed was then twenty-five years of age, of medium height, with broad forehead, large nose slightly hooked, wide mouth with front teeth far apart, black beard and moustache, and dark, but bloodshot eyes. On his back he had a round fleshy tumour of the size of a pigeon's egg; its furrowed surface was covered with hair, and its base was surrounded by black moles; and Sprenger tells us that in later years this was regarded by his followers as the seal of his prophetic mission. But though slightly hump-backed, his appearance must have been on the whole passable.

He fell in with the suggestion of his uncle, and Khadija accepted the offer of his services; and to this circumstance he owed his successful career as a prophet. For Khadija, with womanly instinct, at once appreciated in the dreamy and poetic youth, those finer traits which his own less far-seeing relatives and friends had only despised. She was forty years of age, and it seems strange that she should have been attracted by this uncouth and ignorant youth. Did she foresee glory as the wife of a future Mahdi? She had been twice married and was therefore not unlearned in the art of attracting male affection. She proposed to Mohammed, and perhaps because he had hitherto been too poor to achieve the ambition of every Meccan youth, of setting up a tent for himself, she was accepted.

It is not surprising that her father refused his consent to such a misalliance. But one evening his loving daughter gave him freely of his favourite wine, and whilst he was in a state of intoxication she and Mohammed persuaded him to make them man and wife. And thus was sealed the fate and fortune of the potential prophet. For it was Khadija's encouragement which in the end persuaded him that his revelations were divine and that he was called to the prophetic office.

She bore Mohammed six children, and for years he just lived a prosperous, virtuous, and peaceful family life—peaceful perhaps because he had the habit of withdrawing for considerable periods to the solitude of the bare and desolate Mount Hera, in order that he might pursue his favourite avocation of meditation with prayer and ascetic exercises.

And this is the way in which, according to tradition, Mohammed came to proclaim openly what had long been working within him—in other words, how he became a professed prophet.

Once in the month of Ramadan, when he was about thirty-eight years of age and Khadija was fifty-three, while he was in retreat, wandering on Mount Hera, the Angel Gabriel appeared in the sky, and approaching within two bows' lengths or yet nearer, held before him a silken scroll and compelled him, though he could not read, to recite what stood written on it. And in the words of the Koran, " He revealed to his servant that which he revealed. The heart of Mohammed did not falsely represent that which he saw " (Sura liii).

The words remained graven on his heart. When the angel left him Mohammed came to Khadija, whom he seems to have regarded more as a mother than a wife, and recounted the occurrence in great distress: he thought he was possessed. " O Khadija," he said, " I have never abhorred anything as I do these idols and soothsayers; and now verily I fear lest I should become a soothsayer myself."
" No, never," replied the faithful Khadija, " think of all your many virtues; the Lord would never suffer it thus to be."

Secretly, however, she felt need of confirmation of her

instinct and she repaired to her cousin Waraka, and told him what had occurred. " By the Lord," cried the aged man, " He speaketh Truth ! Doubtless it is the beginning of prophecy, and there shall come upon him the great Namus, like it came upon Moses." And so Khadija comforted Mohammed and confirmed him in the belief that he had received a revelation and was called as a man of God.

But Khadija was jealous for her husband's morals, and would not take on trust the characters of his celestial visitors. And being a practical woman she tested their virtues—in a somewhat original fashion—and we are told that on one occasion, wishing to prove whether the spirit was from God or from the devil, she took Mohammed on her lap and removed her veil, or uncovered her garments, and when the spirit immediately disappeared she knew that it was at any rate possessed of modesty.

Yet because his revelations were not continuous, Mohammed's doubts as to whether they really were from God or from the devil returned, for he deemed it the gravest crime to speak falsely in the name of God, and he was so deeply perplexed and distressed that he was often on the point of seeking death by throwing himself down from the pinnacles of Mount Hera.

This state of anguish continued for two or three years, till one day when he had determined on self-destruction, he was suddenly arrested by hearing a voice which said, " O Mohammed ! Thou art the Prophet of the Lord in truth, and I am Gabriel." Mohammed ran to Khadija in great excitement and cried, " Wrap me up, wrap me up," for this was always done when he fell into trance. Then was sent down another Sura or written revelation, beginning with the words, " Oh thou enveloped one ! Arise and preach ! And magnify thy Lord " (Sura lxxiv). Thenceforth there was no interruption and no doubt ; the revelations continued without a break, and the prophet was assured of his vocation.

Mohammed's inspirations always descended unexpectedly and without warning. He himself, when questioned, said,

"Inspiration cometh in one of two ways: sometimes Gabriel communicateth the revelation to me, as one man to another, and this is easy: at other times it is like the ringing of a bell penetrating my very heart and rending me; and this it is which affecteth me the most." And later Mohammed attributed his grey hairs to the withering effect produced upon him by the " terrific Suras."

And there is no doubt that at any rate in the early years of his inspiration, he believed sincerely and earnestly in the genuineness of his revelations which came to him through Gabriel as messages of God, and were prefaced by the words: " Speak," or " Say," either expressed or understood.

For how otherwise than as inspiration could he who was totally unlearned account for the bursts of eloquence which came to him in his moments of ecstasy? Or whence, if not from Gabriel, came all that ready information always at the tip of his tongue on every subject that presented itself? Surely this had no other source but Gabriel, who had said (Sura xxv), " They shall not come to thee with any strange question but we will bring thee the truth in answer, and a most excellent interpretation."

All this, together with his objective visions of the spirit, whom he knew as Gabriel, were to him unmistakable evidence of supraterrestrial influence. But for the first three years of his mission, Mohammed did not appear as a public preacher. He sought recruits for the cause of Allah in private circles only. He was probably wise thus to experiment privately, for if he could, as he did, convert his wife, his household, and his personal friends, he could convert anything.

But when he began preaching amongst the people and upholding Monotheism, there arose at once enmity between him and the Meccans. For though they might, they said, listen to a prophet such as the Jews and the Christians had found in Moses and in Jesus, they would not listen to a mere preacher. They were in the toils of idolatry and superstition, and would not desert their gods and goddesses.

And this introduces us to a psychic episode which is specially interesting, as it enforces the warning of St. Paul that we must try the spirits to see whether they are or whether they are not of God.

For once when the heads of the tribe of the Koreish were assembled at the Ka'ba,[1] Mohammed came and began to recite one of the Suras, which had been previously revealed to him. But when he came to a certain passage, the devil, or some evil spirit, put in his mouth words which were an admission of the authority of two of the Meccan Goddesses, an admission which Mohammed had long wished to have by revelation from God.

The Meccans were surprised and delighted at this recognition of their deities, and they all with one accord expressed their satisfaction with Mohammed and declared themselves ready to accept him as their prophet.

But Mohammed went home disquieted with his compromise. And in the evening, as he might have expected, there was trouble. Gabriel came to him and asked, " What hast thou done ? Thou hast spoken in the ears of the people words that I never gave to thee."

Mohammed fell in deep distress, fearing to be cast out of the sight of God. But he was taken back to grace, and he revised the reading in a monotheistic sense. So much for compromise, which in religious matters generally is the work of a devil.

Another revelation, in which he was severely censured, came after an occasion when he had turned away from a blind beggar in order to speak to an illustrious man. And—much to his credit—he published this revelation (Sura lxxx).

But the Meccans were intractable, and in the year A.D. 652 he and his followers fled to Medina, for here, at a distance from the Ka'ba, a temple which from the time of Abraham had been a sacred centre for Jewish and for heathen pilgrimages, the people were less intolerant. And before long Mohammed became the most powerful man both politically

[1] Temple said by tradition to have been founded by Abraham.

and spiritually, not only in Medina but also in a much extended sphere.

And at this point our interest in Mohammed ceases, for he soon began to use his increasing moral influence, which he had gained by spiritual means, to enforce his political power, and then sinking to a further stage of degeneration, he relied on his political power to supplement and to confirm his spiritual authority. And, finally, he upheld and sought justification for spiritual, moral, and political power in that which is the last resource of those who have no real moral or spiritual authority—the sword.

In extenuation, however, of his advocacy of the sword, it should perhaps be remembered that as a prophet Mohammed was handicapped as compared with his predecessors whom we have discussed, by the limitations of his psychic faculties. For beyond the power of clairaudience and clairvoyance he seems to have possessed no other means of testifying by supernormal powers the genuineness of his spiritual mandate. He was unable, in short, to perform miracles, and under those circumstances success with the sword would doubtless appear to be the surest credential of divine authority.

He seems to have been deeply conscious of this defect, for the withholding of miracles is referred to several times in the Koran. For instance, in Sura xv we read, " The Meccans say O thou to whom the admonition hath been sent down, thou art certainly possessed with a devil: would'st thou not have come unto us with an attendance of angels, if thou hadst spoken truth ? "

And in reply Mohammed was told to say: " We sent not down the angels, unless on a just occasion, nor should they be then respited any longer. . . . We have heretofore sent Apostles before thee among the ancient sects ; and there came no Apostle unto them, but they laughed him to scorn. . . . If we should open a gate in the Heaven above them, and they should ascend thereto all the day long, they would surely say, Our eyes are only dazzled ; or rather we are a people deluded by enchantments " (Sura xv).

Again in Sura xvii the spirit says, " Nothing hindered us from sending thee with miracles except that the former nations have charged them with imposture. We gave unto the tribe of Thanud at their demand the she-camel visible to their sight ; yet they dealt unjustly with her. . . . We have appointed the vision which we showed thee (a reference to the occasion when Mohammed made his night journey from Mecca to Jerusalem, when he was carried through the seven heavens to the presence of God and brought back again to Mecca the same night—either in vision or in ecstasy or in the astral body). We have appointed also the tree cursed in the Koran only for an occasion of dispute unto men and to strike them with terror ; but it shall cause them to transgress only the more enormously."

Again Gabriel says in Sura xxi, " The Meccans even say the Koran is a confused heap of dreams ; nay he hath forged it ; nay, he is a poet ; let him come unto us, therefore, with some miracle, in like manner as the former prophets were sent. But none of the cities which we have destroyed believed the miracles which they saw performed before them ; will these therefore believe if they see a miracle ? If they should see a fragment of the heaven falling down upon them they would say, It is only a thick cloud " (Sura lii).

But to his followers the Koran was the greatest miracle of all. As Mohammed could not write, the words or revelations, or Suras, as they were called, which were revealed to him by the spirit whom he knew as Gabriel, were taken down by scribes on scrolls or on leaves of palm, and were collected and termed the Koran or the Word of God. Gabriel tells him (Sura xvii), " Say, Verily if men and genii were purposely assembled that they might produce a book like this Koran, they could not produce one like unto it, although the one of them assisted the other."

Even his contemporary adversaries supposed the Koran to be an impossible production for Mohammed, for he had, as Gabriel told him to remind them, dwelt among them for forty years before he received it (Sura x) and had, as his fellow-citizens well knew, never applied himself to learning of any sort, nor frequented learned men, nor had ever exercised himself in composing verses or orations whereby he might acquire the art of rhetoric or elegance of speech. A flagrant proof, says one of his biographers, that this book could be taught him by none but God. And when he insisted, as proof of its divine origin, that it was impossible for a man so unacquainted with learning as himself to have composed such a book, they could only suggest that he had one or more assistants in the forgery.

And Gabriel in reply asks, " Do they say he hath forged the Koran ? . . . Let them produce a discourse like unto it if they speak truth" (Sura lii).

Again : " By the star when it setteth, your companion Mohammed erreth not, nor is he led astray, neither doth he speak of his own will. It is no other than a revelation which hath been revealed unto him. One mighty in power, endued with understanding, taught it him " (Sura liii).

But as illustration of his power of seeing spirit forms a story is told of how on one occasion " A corpse lay in an empty room. Mohammed entered alone, picking his steps carefully as if he walked in the midst of men seated closely on the ground. On being asked the cause, he replied : ' True there were no men in the room, but it was so filled with angels, all seated on the ground, that I found no-where to sit down, until one of the angels spread out his wing for me on the ground, and I sat thereon.' "

Psychic students may also find incidental proof that Mohammed was mediumistic and liable to fall into trance in the fact that his skin, which perspired profusely, is said to have exhaled a strong smell, a phenomenon that is often noted with trance mediums. It is said that devoted followers—and they must indeed have been devoted—found a cure for their ailments in drinking the water in which he had bathed. " And it must," remarks Sprenger dryly, " have been very refreshing."

It is, however, clear that though he had not the psychic

faculty which enabled greater prophets to establish their authority definitely by its means, he had sufficient power of clairvoyance and clairaudience to serve as assurance for himself that he was divinely called and that his teaching concerning God, prayer, and immortality was based upon evidence which was to him conclusive of the existence of the spirit-world.

And it is to be doubted whether at that time and under the special circumstances in which the independent and subdivided tribes of Arabia were then living, any purely political or any purely spiritual influence would have succeeded in accomplishing the miracle which Mohammed performed of welding into a united Whole that disintegrated people. He performed a great work and has exercised in the history of the world a power which will be variously appraised in accordance with men's estimate of the importance to world's morality, as apart from spirituality, of the principle of the equal value of the sexes.

Those who believe that prostitution with its attendant evils is largely the result of a debased status of the female sex will hold Mohammed responsible for having done much to cover with a harem veil of respectability a form of incontinence which, disapproved by greater teachers, is a social canker prohibitive of social or of spiritual progress. Whilst those who are content to proclaim that the two sexes have to-day equal status and that modern prostitution is the result of natural forces which can never be controlled, will lay stress on those aspects of the work of Mohammed from which undoubted benefits accrued, namely, his unification of the broken tribes of Arabia into a political whole ; his presentment of civilization to some millions of human beings who, though they might, but for his forceful teaching, have been led into the Christian fold, yet might on the other hand have remained sunk in barbarism or would not have been raised to that level of brotherhood which Islam not only preaches but also practises.

Unfortunately for his personal reputation his morals degenerated pitiably after the death of Khadija, both in

MOHAMMED

his public and in his private life. When once the firm hand of this capable and sympathetic woman was removed, he gave way to excesses both in public and in private life. In his public life he was guilty of acts of the grossest perfidy, cruelty, and vindictiveness. Amongst other horrors perpetrated by him he caused to be murdered in cold blood, and himself witnessed the crime, eight hundred Jewish prisoners,[1] and he justified it by proclaiming that "the judgment was the judgment of God pronounced on high from beyond the seventh heaven."

And in private life—if life with a large harem can be called private !—he yielded freely to the sensuous passions of an Eastern despot, and although he proclaimed as a sacred message in the Koran (Sura iv) that no man should indulge in more than four wives, his own harem expanded in accordance with his inclinations, till it included ten wives in addition to female slaves or concubines ; nor did he disdain to employ despicable means of attaining the object of his desire ; as, when in defiance of his own Koran, he married for his sixth spouse the wife of his adopted son, who was still alive : and he sanctified this in the eyes of the people by calling down a special revelation.

How, then, the sceptic will ask, can we talk of inspiration ? For he claimed a revelation for all his acts and proclamations. In answer we repeat our opening phrase, that Mohammed is an unfortunate illustration of our thesis. He was inspired, possibly throughout his life, from the spirit-world, and so long as he himself was single-hearted in his purpose, he drew to his side spirits who guided him aright. But from the moment that motives of a worldly egoistic and power-acquiring type pervaded his mind, he became the prey of lesser spirits, or possibly, if through sensuousness he lost his psychic faculty, he may have supplied from his own subjective imagination what he could no longer obtain as objective revelation.

But—he was undoubtedly a great Teacher and a great power in the world for good or ill—his followers even to-day

[1] Sir W. Muir, p. 319.

number roughly 120 millions, and are spread over three continents, and he undoubtedly derived his primary authorization as a teacher directly from the spirit-world by means of his supernormal faculties of clairvoyance and clairaudience.

Therefore, though he was on a lower spiritual plane than the other Teachers whom we have named, he is yet an illustration of our argument that psychic phenomena have been the inspiration of every great religious Teacher.

JOAN OF ARC
(A.D. 1412)

IN all history, sacred or secular, there is probably no story which better illustrates the influence of the psychic faculty on those who have been leaders of men than the story of the Maid of Orleans.

The story is in a sense well known, but amongst the general public it has never been appreciatively understood, mainly because the psychic gifts which enabled Joan to carry out her work have not been understood. Even the latest dramatic representation of this wonderful tale is robbed of its intrinsic interest by the author's lack of comprehension of the source of the Maid's power. Bernard Shaw, in the preface to his play, *St. Joan*, regards her as an " impudent young upstart," with " unwomanly and insufferable presumption." He says that " her voices never gave Joan any advice that might not have come to her from her mother wit, exactly as gravitation came to Newton." That " she worked by common sense." That " her voices and visions were illusory, and their wisdom all Joan's own." Then, feeling that mere denial of the supernormality of the occurrences was unworthy of the Shavian intellect, he gives an interpretation of the phenomena of Joan's visions which is pure logomachy. He says that, " the figure Joan recognized as St. Catherine . . . was the dramatization by Joan's imagination of that pressure upon her of the driving force that is behind evolution "—a sentence which is mere intellectual buffoonery to those of us who have come in contact with phenomena of a type similar to the visions experienced by Joan.

But notwithstanding the scepticism of Bernard Shaw, Joan is, little by little, coming into her own, for she is at least to-day acknowledged as a Saint, not, however, in accordance with the Shavian recognition, which says that " A saint is a person of heroic virtue whose private judgment is privileged." Joan was at last recognized as a Saint because she combined "heroic virtue" with the exercise of supernormal gifts, by means of which she acquired wisdom, authority, and power to carry out her work.

Now there are only three possible interpretations of the phenomena which characterized Joan's career. These phenomena were either, (*a*) as Bernard Shaw believes, illusory, or (*b*) they were, as the Church of her day believed, of the devil, or (*c*) they were illustrations of the exercise of psychic gifts—of clairvoyance, clairaudience, and divination—of a type familiar to and verifiable by psychic scientists to-day, gifts which were by Joan used in communicating with holy spirits who inspired the Maid to her stupendous mission.

For Joan herself there was only one interpretation. The divine source of her inspiration was never for a moment in doubt. " I come," she proclaimed everywhere, " from the King of Heaven, and I will bring you the help of Heaven." And she did.

But let us now briefly recall the main incidents of Joan's life that we may judge for ourselves whether we are not justified in believing that Joan became famous as a great leader on account of her psychic powers, and that we are therefore justified in including this great heroine in our series.

Joan, who is described by Conan Doyle as the most spiritual being next to the Christ (Preface to the *Mystery of Joan of Arc*, by Léon Denis, translated by A. Conan Doyle), was born of poor parents in the village of Domrémy in the East of France, in the year 1412, during times that were full of misery for her country. There was no League of Nations to interfere, and the English King, Henry V, on pretext of having married the French Princess, Katherine, was engaged in the task of " conquering France." The French themselves were, curiously enough, divided in their sympathies, mainly owing to the indolence, imbecility, and indecision of the Dauphin Charles, and throughout the country plunder, rapine, and confusion were rampant.

Now Joan was of a thoughtful and religious temperament. She loved solitude, and impressed by the thought of her country's sufferings, she used to go by herself to lonely places to pray God to have pity on France. At the age of thirteen she was a strong, handsome, well-made girl, with thick, dark hair—in the words of a young knight, The Count Guy de Laval, who was describing her in a letter to his mother: " a creature all divine."

But she was not merely a sentimental dreamer, she must have been a normally healthy and athletic child; for one day she and some other girls and boys in her village were running a race for a garland of flowers, and she was easily the winner. And for psychic students this race has a special interest, for as Joan was running, another child who was looking on cried out, " Joan, I see you flying along without touching the ground."[1] Was this perhaps the " pressure upon her " of the driving force that is behind evolution, or was it not quite simply a form of levitation well understood by psychic students, a form of unconscious levitation similar to that which on a certain occasion, as we shall later see, disconcerted St. Teresa during a service in the choir of a church?

After the race, Joan seemed to be in a trance, and she heard a voice which told her to go home as her mother needed her.

Another day she was standing about midday in her father's garden, when she saw a bright light, like a shining cloud, as she described it, and an angelic figure, a spirit-voice spoke, and told her to be a good girl and go to church —and go to save France. Though she was at first afraid, she replied quite sensibly that she was only a poor girl who could not ride or lead the soldiers in the wars. However, for years the voice kept on telling her that she must go.

And that the voices she heard were not merely imaginary,

[1] *The Story of Joan of Arc*, Andrew Lang.

within her own mind as the result of common sense, but were heard by her as objective external phenomena, is shown by the fact that she could not hear them distinctly when there was much noise in the room.

She not only continuously heard these voices but she saw shining figures of spirits whom she called saints, as clearly as she saw people. She used to cry when they went away and she wished that they would take her with them. She identified her three chief spirit guides—and quite naturally —under the names of the three saints, Catherine, Margaret, and Michael, whose statues stood in the little church at Domrémy, where she went every day to pray. And later she had, she said, a whole council of angels who advised her in everything.

Time went on and the Dauphin's cause had become desperate. He only held France south of the Loire. Orleans was the strongest place still in his hands, and if the English succeeded in taking that, he would be driven from France and the English would have possession of his country.

But the indolent and self-indulgent Dauphin, without will-power or determination, did nothing but wander about from one place to another amusing himself, and, in true twentieth-century fashion, holding endless councils in attractive places.

And far away in that little village of Domrémy Joan heard from time to time of the danger in which Orleans, the last French stronghold, stood, and the voices grew more and more insistent and told her that she must go and drive away the English.

This seemed to Joan a perfectly mad proposal. How could a little peasant girl of sixteen, who couldn't read or write, or ride or fight, teach the French how to defeat the English? She used to cry because she said people would think she was mad or bad and that they would only laugh at her. But the voices became more definite, and they began instructing her as to what she was to do and where she was to go. Then the saints and angels and the shining cloud came several times every week, and at last a voice said, "Daughter of God, you will lead the Dauphin to Rheims to be consecrated." And finally came the imperative words, "Daughter of God, go on, I will be with you."

There was now no help for it. And one day this little peasant child of sixteen summers calmly left her village home—not to go to a neighbouring fair, but to drive the English army out of France. And she succeeded.

By what means? By what means alone could this supernormal feat have been accomplished? Her first success was certainly due to her power of clairvoyance. She was on her way to Chinon to see the Dauphin, in accordance with spirit instructions, and the commander of the town of Vaucouleur, through which she had to pass, refused to give her an escort. But one day she heard clairaudiently from her voices that a great disaster (the Battle of the Herrings) had befallen the Dauphin's army near Orleans.

She told the Commander of this, and when a few days later this prediction was verified, the Commander realized that there must be something uncommon about this country girl who could tell what was happening miles away. So he lent her some men-at-arms to guide and guard her on her way. That encouraged somebody else to give her a horse, and to the surprise of everybody she was able to ride it very well.

She then exchanged her red skirt for a grey doublet and black hose, cut her long hair short, and after days of continuous riding she and her little company reached Chinon where the Dauphin was.

The Dauphin's advisers were doubtful as to whether he ought to see the Maid, but in the end possibly curiosity prevailed, and she was brought to the castle and led up the stairs to a great hall in which were assembled a company of about three hundred knights and noble ladies in magnificent dresses.

One man only was plainly dressed, and directly Joan saw him she went up to him and kneeling on one knee, she said, "Fair Sir, you are the Dauphin to whom I am come." He, however, hoping to deceive her, pointed to another knight

who was richly dressed and said, " No—that is the King."
" No, Fair Sir," said Joan. " It is to you that I am sent."

The Dauphin was much impressed, but it was only a day or two later that she made him definitely believe in her. She seized an opportunity to take him aside, and she then whispered in his ear something which was to him startling evidence of her supernormal knowledge. She reminded him of a secret prayer he had once made, asking that he might know whether he really was the son of the late King, and therefore the rightful King of France, as there was doubt as to his legitimacy. " And you are the rightful King," said Joan.

The Dauphin was so stirred that he sent priests to Joan's village to make inquiries as to her reputation; then, as this was unimpeachable, she was taken to Poitiers to be examined by learned men, priests and lawyers. They all tried, but in vain, to confuse her by their questions. She was straightforward in her answers and told them exactly how the voices came to her. And she showed a mental dexterity and wit that were certainly abnormal in this uneducated girl, for though, as she told them, she did not know A from B, " I read," she said, " in a book where are more things than are found in yours."

Then they wanted her to work a miracle, but she told them she was not there for such a purpose; she was there to lead an army to Orleans.

At last, after six weary weeks, the learned men and priests, who had tried in every way to entangle her, drew up and signed a report in which they, as learned men judging on the spot after weeks of experimentation, confessed that " To doubt the Maid, would be to resist the Holy Spirit."

The Dauphin then at last did what he should have done long ago, he collected an army to march with Joan to Orleans. Thenceforth, clad in white armour, this girl of sixteen led the army, riding or running, always in front of them, through a rain of arrows, bullets, and cannon balls, waving her banner of Christ and the Lilies of France, and crying, " Come on."

JOAN OF ARC

Many and various were her clairvoyant and true predictions of events during this time. One of the most interesting, which is reminiscent of the Glastonbury romance, was her prediction that if they would dig behind the altar in the chapel of St. Catherine at Fierbois, they would find a buried sword which had been placed there by Charles Marcel. She wished to carry this sword. It was thus found, old and rusty, with five crosses on the blade.

The account of Joan's military exploits can, of course, be read in many books, but briefly summarized this peasant girl, who knew nothing of soldiering or of tactics, out-generalled the French Generals, and not only put fresh heart, courage, and confidence into the disorganized army, but planned and succeeded in strategies where the best French Army brains had hitherto failed.

Although herself wounded, she succeeded in four days in delivering the town of Orleans, which for seven months had been besieged by the English. That was on the 8th of May. On the 11th of June she took the town of Jargeau. On the 15th she took Meun. On the 17th Beaugency, and on the 18th she destroyed Talbot's chief army at Pathay, and on the 17th of July the Dauphin was crowned at Rheims.

Surely all this was beyond the normal human powers of an unlettered country girl, and was due not to any worldly knowledge of military tactics, but to power derived from a supernormal source. That was at least Joan's conviction. For instance, on one occasion, when most of the French had retired out of shot from a breach in the walls, she was left almost alone with a very small company. When urged not to remain there longer alone, she took off her helmet and said, " I am not alone ; here I have with me 50,000 of my own "—meaning, of course, her invisible army of angels—" and I will not leave this place till I take the town." And she took it.

In short, the four tasks which she had set herself, or which had been set for her by her spirit guides, she successfully accomplished. These were : To drive the English in flight : to crown the King at Rheims : to deliver Orleans : and to set free the Duke of Orleans, who was a prisoner in England.

And but for the shameful dilatoriness and the treachery of the King and his advisers, who amongst their other follies refused to follow up the Coronation by marching on Paris, she would have done much more. For though in miraculous manner she had unified France, made of it a nation, and had rescued the country from domination by a foreign power, the English were not completely driven from France till twenty years later.

And surely the fact that 10,000 men, soldiers, and officers, should have consented to be led by this young and untrained girl, was of all the other miracles the most miraculous. In her campaign on the Loire, says Léon Denis, the Generals Dunois, La Hire, Gaucourt, and Xaintrailles marched under the orders of this girl of eighteen.

But now comes the tragic and to some people the inexplicable part of this great story. From the beginning she had known from her spirit guides that her power would only last a year, and she had, for this amongst other reasons, continually implored the worthless and dilatory Dauphin to give up dallying and holding futile councils and to be more active : she was therefore not unprepared when in Easter week suddenly the voices of St. Catherine and St. Margaret spoke and told her that she would be taken prisoner before midsummer day ; that thus it must needs be ; that she was to be resigned to her fate ; and that God would help her.

Thenceforth she received no further help from her voices, who merely reiterated the announcement that she would be captured. Joan knew that this meant being burnt alive, but she continued her divine mission with a faith and with a courage greater than even before, since she was now left to her own human resources, and was every day exposing herself to the danger, not of death from sword or bullet, which she would have welcomed, but to the most horrible of all deaths—death by torturing flames.

JOAN OF ARC

In a rash and desperate sally to relieve the town of Compiègne, which was surrounded by the English and the Burgundians, she was captured. Hoping for death by the sword, she refused to surrender, saying, " I have given my faith to another than you, and I will keep my oath to Him."

Her captors, however, hoping to replete exhausted coffers, refrained from killing her outright ; they offered her to the French in exchange for £10,000, and to the everlasting disgrace of her countrymen these refused to pay the ransom. The Duke of Luxembourg, into whose hands she fell, then sold her for this sum to the English—to be burnt alive.

The fiendish cruelty of the English and the treachery and ingratitude of the French, whose country she had rescued after a war which had lasted for a hundred years, seem to us to-day to be traits of human character almost unbelievable. It is true that the Church and France have at last made a scant and tardy reparation for a crime which can never be expunged. They have now transferred their great heroine, acclaimed by Southey to be the greatest heroine of the human race, from the status of a witch to that of a Saint : but chiefly it is to be feared because it seems more reputable for the glory of their country that France should have received her salvation at the hands of a saint reputed to have been honoured by divine favour, rather than through the agency of a common witch.

It is also to be feared that the Churches both in France and in England have not learned the general lesson which Joan's life and death should teach. For what was the cause of the displeasure of the Church towards Joan ? Was it not purely and simply this, that Joan dared to assert that her authority came direct from Heaven and not through the channel of the Church ?

" Are you willing," asked a Bishop at her trial, " to submit to the Church ? "

" I refer all things to God, and God has always inspired me," was Joan's answer.

" This is a grave saying," retorted the Bishop. " Between you and God there stands the Church."

And is this not the same sentiment, expressed or unexpressed, which influences the Churches in their attitude towards psychical research to-day ? Is not the antagonism of the Churches towards psychic science largely based upon the fear that men might find their salvation and derive authority for their beliefs direct from Heaven, instead of through the agency of the Church ?

With Joan, with Socrates, with Christ, is it not always the same struggle between tradition which has become crystallized into law on the one side, and individual inspiration on the other ? And do not the upholders of religious tradition invariably forget that their traditions started life as inspiration ? The sequence is invariably the same: inspiration memorialized becomes religion, and religion ecclesiasticized fades into tradition, which is then artificially kept alive by Law.

And so for all those individual souls who crave communion with their God, each in accordance with his own special needs, the Church blocks the way, for she declares that there is only one door of communication between man and God, and that is the narrow portal of the Church, through which only a limited number can pass. And those who believe that there is no other way, give up religion in despair. Effectively, indeed, too often " between man and God there stands the Church."

But why, it may be asked, was it ordained that Joan should suffer this cruel death if her spiritual guides were in control of her fate ? Why was it that her saints and angels did not come to the rescue and save this pure and saintly girl from such fiendish torture ?—for she was, as we all know, at the age of nineteen, in the year of our Lord 1431, burnt alive as an evil witch in the market place of Rouen, her stake surrounded by eight hundred soldiers to prevent any possibility of escape.

In reply, two thoughts suggest themselves. Firstly, that we earthly folk grossly exaggerate the importance of our earthly bodies and that we are probably quite mistaken in supposing death—which is really re-birth—to be a disaster. Secondly: it was in Joan's case, as in others of which we are cognizant, the sacrifice of her life which riveted her story upon the imagination of the world. Had Joan outlived the special work for which she was selected: had she died a " natural " death, as a toothless and derelict old woman, the story of her supernormal exploits and the proof these afford of psychic powers might never have passed into universal history.

And we must remember that Joan's voices when they warned her of her fate, told her that God would help her. This meant, we may presume, that she would be shielded from all suffering. Now we know that many psychic subjects can handle fire with impunity, and therefore we may be sure that Joan would certainly thus have been protected.

But we are here concerned, not in attempting to find justification for the ways of Providence, but in pointing out that had our humble little Joan not possessed psychic faculties, the idea that she could save her country from a foreign foe would never have entered into her head, and that but for those exceptional psychic faculties, but for the fact that she was a great medium, she would never have succeeded.

ST. TERESA
(A.D. 1515)

PEOPLE talk very glibly about " the Saints " of the Church. But what is a saint ? What is it that has in most cases differentiated a canonized saint from ordinary virtuous men and women leading self-sacrificing and ascetic lives ? Is it not the characteristic which has distinguished all the religious leaders whom we have here had under review, namely, the psychic faculty, which not only gave wisdom, authority, and confidence to the recipients of the visions and revelations, but which enabled them to prove to the multitude by signs and wonders of a supernormal order that they had received a heavenly mandate.

But rather than admit belief in the objective reality of phenomena of a metapsychic order, many biographers of the saints and of religious leaders, because they have themselves no knowledge of psychic possibilities, resort to metaphysical explanations which are utterly unconvincing. Bernard Shaw's definition of a saint as " a person of heroic virtue whose private judgment is privileged " is flagrantly wide of the mark, specially in the case of Joan of Arc, whom he was then discussing. For why should the private judgment of a peasant girl of sixteen years of age—upon military matters of which she had no normal knowledge—have been regarded as privileged by the foremost generals of the day, unless they had recognized in that private judgment a supernormal influence ?

Similarly, in her *Life of Santa Teresa*—the completest and most interesting and fascinating life that has been

ST. TERESA

written of the Saint, and from which the facts here to be mentioned have been almost exclusively and quite ruthlessly extracted, Gabriela Cunninghame Graham shows no knowledge of the potentialities of the psychic sense, and she resorts therefore to unsatisfying sophisms to cover her ignorance and to excuse the supposed weaknesses of her heroine.

But her case is more pitiful even than that of Bernard Shaw, for she writes two large volumes in which her aim is to extol Teresa as a woman and as a saint, and she fails to realize that Teresa would never have been heard of as a woman or have been canonized as a saint, if it had not been for her visions and her revelations which gave her power and influence as a woman, and which provided that proof of divine favour essential for saintship.

And can the opinion of one who knows nothing of the laws controlling the phenomena under discussion, and who is divided by three centuries from the evidence available, be pitted against the beliefs of those who were on the spot, and who, far from being credulous, were jealous of the phenomena, and were only finally obliged to accept them as supernormal when all other possible explanations had failed, and when circumstantial proofs of their validity were overwhelming?

This biographer is indeed in a quaint quandary, for she stresses throughout the volumes the superior intellect and the exceptional honesty of Teresa, and she is therefore unable to attribute the supernormal phenomena which are described in the saint's own words either to hysteria, to illusion, or to fraud; the explanation we are afforded is that "All who will can have visions—any hysterical girl or distraught woman; the imitators of Teresa number thousands; but how many have described them with the pen of a genius which invests all it touches with interest?"

We are therefore meant to assume that there was nothing remarkable in the phenomena which were the characteristic feature of the life of Teresa, but that these phenomena have subsequently assumed an interest on account of the literary charm by which they were invested by the pen of a clever woman.

That Teresa was a clever woman is undoubted. In argument she was too much for some of her contemporaries. "God help me," exclaimed one Bishop, "I would rather argue with all the theologians in the world put together than with this woman."

But let those who have had experience of psychic phenomena, under conditions when possibility of hysteria, fraud, or illusion was excluded, judge for themselves as to the origin of the mystic experiences of the Spanish saint of Avila in Castile.

We have chosen Teresa almost at haphazard from amongst a large selection of Saints of the Middle Ages both male and female, whose lives would illustrate our purpose, but we would point out that what is characteristic of Teresa is characteristic also, with variations, of most of the saints in the Calendar.

Her name in Greek, Tarasia, was in itself a happy coincidence, for it signifies "marvellous." She was born in the year 1515 of an illustrious old Spanish family. And—let us break the news at once—Teresa was not a natural saint. Some people cannot help being saints, they have no aptitude for anything else. But it took Teresa eighteen years to attain sanctity, and then no one would have been any the wiser and there would have been nothing to differentiate her from thousands of other pious women of her day—piety was the only occupation for women in Spain in those days—if it had not been for her visions and her voices which gave her notoriety and which attracted the curiosity even of the Inquisition.

Her mother died when she, Teresa, was a young girl, beautiful, clever, witty, and in every way attractive. She was not unaware of her charms and she seems to have made the most of them, with the result that her father, to safeguard her from an undesirable love-episode, placed her in a convent.

ST. TERESA

But that did not help matters, as in those days convents seem to have been anything but conventual, and Teresa was much distracted from pious practices by friendships with the young gallants of Avila, who apparently were allowed to use the Convent as a pleasurable afternoon lounge.

For a time Teresa tried to enjoy both God and Mammon; she had a magnetic charm which none could resist, and she knew it, and it was possible that she might have given herself altogether to Mammon, but—she had moments of remorse, and in prayer she began to be conscious of a Presence and of a Voice which constantly admonished her.

She soon found herself living in a supernormal world, and fearing that this might be a snare of the devil she at last unburdened her soul, not to her own Confessor, she did not dare do that, but to a Jesuit priest. Only, however, with hesitation, for, as she naïvely confessed, "she was afraid lest she might be forced to change and to leave her amusements."

The priest, however, showed a rare discretion; and he bade her take courage, for that possibly through her the Lord intended to do good to many. From that moment, under his guidance, she strode forward on the thorny path of mortification and penance from which she had hitherto stood aloof.

She wore next the skin a tin shirt pierced with holes like a grater, which left wounds wherever it touched; she rolled herself in her bed of briers, with as much delight, says Graham, as if it had been a bed of roses; she scourged herself with nettles and with keys till the walls of her cell were splashed with blood; and once when she was ill with fever, she scourged herself till she broke her arm.

But she still found difficulty in breaking off the undesirable friendships and intimacies which were tormenting her conscience, and she describes in her autobiography how it was that she at last acquired the necessary strength of will Here, again, it was a Jesuit priest whose tact and insight into her spiritual psychology smoothed for her the rough path of renunciation. "He told me," she says, "to commend it to God for a few days, and to repeat the hymn, Veni Creator, that I might be given light as to what was best." "After having been deep in prayer one day, and supplicating the Lord to help me to please Him in everything, I began the hymn, and whilst I was saying it, I was seized with a rapture so sudden that it almost carried me beside myself, and of this I could not doubt, for it was very palpable. It was the first time that the Lord had done me this favour. I heard these words, 'I no longer wish thee to converse with men, but with angels.' "

That was enough for Teresa. Thenceforward, even if she would, she found herself unable to love or to take pleasure in the society of those who were not trying to serve God.

This was the first of that series of "divine locutions," as she called them, which thenceforth became constant and were the controlling forces in her life.

One of the most interesting of her experiences was perhaps her vision of the Christ. She describes how at first she felt rather than saw Him, but the cloud-like enveloping Presence, which for some days never left her, gradually became more defined, till one day, she being in prayer, the Lord showed her His Hands—His Hands alone, "with such exceeding beauty as is beyond the power of words to describe." "A few days afterwards," she continued, "I also saw the Divine Face, which left me entirely absorbed in wonder and admiration."

"I could not understand," she says, "why the Lord showed Himself thus by slow degrees." Being ignorant of the laws controlling such phenomena she supposed it was in deference to her human weakness, whereas we to-day can understand that this was a gradual "building up" depending for its completion on the power of the medium through whose psychic faculty the spirit was able to materialize.

And accordingly, as we might expect, these partial

materializations led up to a perfect vision of the full figure which "overwhelmed her with its radiant beauty—not a splendour that dazzles, but a soft whiteness infused with radiance . . . like a very clear stream running over crystal"—a wonderful description of the light with which a materialized spirit shines—"though at times it was," she says "confused"—again a realistic description of attempted materializations when the conditions are not favourable.

Teresa was also liable to the phenomena known to-day as levitation. One of her Confessors, a learned theologian of the Order of St. Dominic, testified to the fact that on one occasion when the saint was attending a service in the choir of a church, she suddenly felt herself being raised from the ground, and she was obliged to seize hold of a rail to prevent levitation, whilst she prayed "Lord suffer not for such a favour, a wicked woman to pass for virtuous" (Fielding Ould's *Wonders of the Saints*). She herself says, "Sometimes my whole body was carried with my soul, so as to be raised from the ground: but this was seldom. When I wished to resist these raptures, there seemed to be somewhat of such mighty force under my feet, which raised me up, that I knew not what to compare it to."

This phenomenon of levitation was not unfrequent amongst saints. St. Francis was often levitated, also St. Ignatius Loyola, St. Philip Neri, St. Joseph Cupertino, St. James of Illyricum, St. Dominic, St. Dunstan, St. Philip Benite, St. Cajetan, St. Albert of Sicily, and St. Bernard Ptolomaei, St. Edmund, Archbishop of Canterbury, Jamblisuc, and St. Thomas Aquinas.

Psychic students, though they are still in doubt as to the means by which the feat of levitation is accomplished, have no doubt as to the possibility of its accomplishment, and Dr. Crawford's scientific experiments have done much to elucidate the phenomena. It has been witnessed in recent years, notably in the persons of the famous medium Daniel D. Home (see Sir William Barrett's *On the Threshhold of the Unseen*) and of William Stainton Moses (see his *Modern Mystics and Modern Magic*, Fielding Ould).

And withal Teresa would have made a creditable member of the Psychical Research Society, for her keen intellect criticized all her experiences with a view to distinguishing positive phenomena from subjective hallucinations and from unconscious mental forgery, and in true scientific manner she gives her reasons for believing that her revelations were objective, and for her assertion that "in spite of all resistance, it is impossible to fail to understand them."

As we can well imagine, it soon became impossible to conceal from the outside world the marvellous experiences of this Carmellite Nun. They created jealousy and ill-will within the Convent, for, as she expresses it with her usual forcefulness, "the Friar and the Nun who in very truth begin to follow their vocation, have more to fear from those of their own community than from all the devils combined."

They also created excitement and much criticism outside the Convent walls, and she became an object of general observation. The painful element in all this for Teresa was the belief at first entertained by the priests and others that these visions and revelations were of the devil. Convinced of their true origin, she suffered martyrdom in having to make the gesture of exorcism with the cross in her hand. And one day, when she thus held out the Crucifix of her rosary, the Christ took it from her fingers; and when she received it back again the four large beads of black ebony were transmuted into precious stones of exceeding brilliancy, and on them were graven the five wounds " of very lovely workmanship."

It is thus clear that Teresa was undoubtedly a great medium, who was not only, like Socrates, clairaudient and constantly admonished by spirit voices, but that she was gifted with a variety of psychic powers. She was continually liable to trances, and often on inconvenient occasions, for sometimes when it was her turn to be on duty in the convent kitchen as cook, she would be found " absorbed in ecstasy," as it was then termed, "unconscious, her face wrapt and

ST. TERESA

beautiful, her rigid hands grasping the frying-pan," for, as she herself remarked, " God walks even among the pots and pipkins."

Her writings, which are acknowledged to be works of genius, she believed to be directly inspired, and this is the view taken by the Roman Catholic Church, which believes that her books were written under the direct inspiration of the Holy Spirit. Teresa says that " Many things of which she wrote were not of her own head, but were the inspiration of her Celestial Master." Whilst she was " rapt away," " her pen," she said, " was guided by a higher power to set down conceptions which were not her own, and whose aptness filled her with wondering astonishment."

This is an experience with which those who make a study of these matters are daily becoming more conversant, and it is easy to understand and to sympathize with her feelings when she exclaimed, " Oh! that I could write with many hands so that some of them (thoughts) were not forgotten," —uttered when dictation from the controlling spirit was more rapid than the human mind and pen could follow.

Indeed, all that we are told about the circumstances attending her writings accords with all that occurs under modern conditions in inspirational writing to-day. " When she wrote," says a Prioress, " it was with such rapidity and without stopping to erase or correct, that it indeed appeared miraculous." " Also her face was illumined," says this same witness, " by a glorious light, which gave forth a splendour like rays of gold, and lasted for an hour, until twelve at night, at which time Teresa ceased to write, and the resplendence faded away from her, leaving her in what, in comparison with it, seemed like darkness."

Graham says that others also who had seen her in the act of composing her great works, maintained that at those moments her face was illumined by an unearthly splendour, as of one in colloquy with the Holy Ghost.

But even more interesting than the evidence given of Teresa's inspirational writing, is an example of direct spirit-writing, which Graham is not able to differentiate from the inspirational or automatic writing. For one night, when a certain Maria del Nacimiento came into Teresa's cell to deliver a message, she saw some sheets of blank paper on which Teresa had just begun to write. But in the very act of taking off her spectacles to attend to the message Teresa was " carried away in an ecstasy " (went into a trance). When she came to herself Maria del Nacimiento noted with amazement that the sheets of paper which before were blank were now covered with handwriting. Whereupon Teresa, desirous to prevent her from seeing what had occurred, threw the " Miraculous MS. with simulated carelessness into a little coffer beside her."

Now to spiritualists this was an intelligible phenomenon known as direct spirit-writing—writing similar to that which appeared on the wall in the palace at the feast of Belshazzar, similar also to the spirit-writing given to Moses on the tables of stone, writing which was, we are told, written by the finger of God. But this is Graham's comment on the experience of Teresa : " Strange that those who hold that Teresa was but an instrument played on by Divine Inspiration should fail to perceive how a hypothesis resting on such slight and intangible evidence—or rather no evidence at all—lessens and belittles her real greatness, and transforms a lofty and original intellect into a mere automatic machine ! "

But what is " real greatness " ? Surely to be used as a medium for the transmission of divine truths is to be more really great than to write clever books dictated by the restricted physical intellect. To those who have never studied psychic phenomena, such happenings must necessarily be incomprehensible, and we can but marvel at the courage of writers like G. Graham or like Bernard Shaw, who select as subjects for their biographies, or their dramas, heroes and heroines whose distinguishing characteristic is the exercise of a faculty of which the writers have not only had no experience, but of which they even deny the existence. Graham, for instance, introduces her readers to the first of Teresa's " divine locutions " by saying : " It is into this mysterious region of her mind peopled with the phantoms and spectres which she herself placed there by some strange psychological process, which must for ever remain unexplained and unexplainable, her own creations which imposed themselves upon her as tangible realities, that we are now about to enter."

But for those who have been privileged to witness phenomena of a nature similar to any of those here recorded, there is nothing, even in the episode of the precious stones, which is unbelievable, or which is not in accordance with laws which are now being scientifically investigated. The only mystery is contained in the strange fact that intelligent people are not tumbling over each other to investigate for themselves phenomena of such supreme importance and of such truly magical interest.

For these psychic phenomena of the physical order are the lower rungs of the ladder which leads from earth to heaven, and though these lower rungs, these physical phenomena, are useless, worse than useless, unless they are taken as steps to a higher ascent, we must never forget that this Jacob's ladder of communication, if we are to ascend it, must of necessity start from earth. It would be of no use to us worldly mortals if it were poised in mid-air. Psychic phenomena of the physical order are in short a means to an end, but they must never be confounded with that end which is—Revelation, pure Revelation of the Will of God to man.

We to-day want to know, not only what God said to Moses, living three or four thousand years ago, though that is of intense interest, nor even what God had to say to Christ, living 1900 odd years ago, though that is all-important. We want to know what God has to say to us who are living in the twentieth century. We want to learn not only how to find our friends on the plane beyond, we want to learn how to find God, that we may learn, as Teresa learnt, direct from Him, through His spirit messengers, what He would have us to do in these difficult, complicated, and materialistic times. And unless we seek we shall never find : and unless we knock—and by ways approved by all the great Initiates of old—the gates of Heaven will not unfold.

But to return to Teresa. It was a vision of hell which finally determined her to devote her life to a practical cause, namely, to the rescue of souls and to the extirpation of heresy.

And it is encouraging for those of active temperament, who crave a greater knowledge of religion, to realize that all the greatest religious leaders in world-history, have not allowed their zeal and enthusiasm to fizzle out in sanctimonious solitude, but have been hard workers in fields of practical service.

And so Teresa, who suffered from execrable health, and laboured under the disadvantages of being a mere woman in an age when woman's sphere was restricted to the home and to the convent, Teresa, when she was already over middle-age, undertook the reform of the Carmellite Order, which had, as she knew from bitter experience, fallen into extreme laxity of discipline. To effect this, she organized in remote parts of the country new Foundations—at San José, Malagon, Duruelo, Toledo, Pastrana, Salamanca, Alba de Tornes—foundations which were, in antithesis to those already in existence, dedicated to poverty. And she encountered, of course, every conceivable kind of difficulty, social, financial, and physical.

To understand fully the extent of her work and the reform which she initiated in the Order of the Carmellites, and through example in all the religious Orders of the day, Teresa's arduous toil and apparently miraculous ways of overcoming difficulties must be followed by our readers in G. Graham's two fine volumes. Her work, as will then be realized, was gigantic, and the point of this essay is that this work was only made possible when, after a time, it came to be recognized that her visions and her revelations, far from being visitations of the devil, were marks of divine favour. Then her fame spread abroad even to the Courts, and Kings and Princes flocked to see her. They came,

ST. TERESA

however, not to extol her virtues, but to marvel at her miracles, and thus she gained the prestige and the influence which together with an indomitable will and a great intellect, enabled her, in spite of her miserable health, to overcome all the obstacles in her path.

This is acknowledged by Graham, who says: "Nevertheless it was to her visions that she owed that prominence without which she must have lived and died an obscure nun in an obscure Castilian Convent. It was her visions and revelations which first gained for her that character for sanctity, without which it would have been impossible for her even to dream of undertaking the work which was to be the idea and dominating reason of her life. She might have practised for ever, swallowed up in the shadow of the Enarancion, all the heroic virtues of the Christian, and no one a whit the wiser that a rare flower had blossomed in and spread its fragrance through those sun-lit cloisters."

But Teresa's psychic faculties assisted her in this work not only socially, morally, and financially, but also physically. Time after time this elderly nun of the feeblest health was enabled to overcome the difficulties attendant on journeying in rough carts over Castilian mountain tracks, and in crossing flooded and bridgeless rivers, by direct supernormal means, as for instance when on her way to Medina she and her companions were guided to the opposite bank of a flooded river by a light held by unseen hands—a psychic light, no doubt similar to that which is familiar to students of metapsychic phenomena, and which is in reality no miracle, but a manifestation of a power inherent in those who are truly mediums of communication between two planes of existence.

But Teresa is an interesting example of the fact that in order to succeed as a leader in the realm of religion, a rare combination of qualities is required—a combination, namely, of morality, spirituality, will, and intellect, plus the psychic faculty. Those who have morality alone remain philanthropists: those who have spirituality alone remain monks or hermits: those with will power alone remain Napoleons in the various spheres of work : those who have intellect alone remain scientists : whilst those who have psychic power alone remain mediums. And though an association of any of these qualities minus the psychic faculty may produce Leaders who are great in more than one sphere of life, the addition of the psychic faculty to these others is essential in the creation of a great religious Leader. Only those who combine with morality, spirituality, will, and intellect the great gift of superconsciousness, of a cosmic consciousness, which enables them to penetrate a higher plane of thought, become religious geniuses, reformers, saints, or prophets, and founders of religion.

And presumably it is for this reason that great religious leaders have been so sparingly distributed throughout the history of the world because to all these other qualities must be adjoined the possession—and in superlative degree—of that disused and generally atrophied psychic sense which is alas now diagnosed as supernormal.

Teresa died in 1582 at the age of sixty-seven, at the height of her fame, and it is not surprising to learn that a great and brilliant throng of celestial spirits surrounded her deathbed. Nor is it altogether surprising if, as is asserted, miracles, so-called, should have been worked by her dead body.

It was, for instance, attested by many that after her death, as well as during her life, a strange fragrance emanated from her. This is a phenomenon which was not peculiar to Teresa, it is found in certain stages of trance in many mediums. And is this not possibly the origin of the phrase " to die in the odour of sanctity " ?

It was also universally asserted that her body never knew corruption. It was several times exhumed and cruelly mutilated for purposes of relics, and the flesh was said to be still fair and unchanged.

And now in reading the story of how, in an age when women were expected to be neither seen nor heard, this rail woman, with execrable health, overcame all the difficulties—which are clearly set out in Graham's *Life*—and accomplished her great work, are we not believing the less miraculous of two alternative opinions if instead of believing with her biographer, that she achieved her goal and attained her canonization by virtue of intellect and piety alone, we admit that it was her psychic revelations which made her famous, which gave her the prestige and influence essential to the inauguration and financing of her work, and which in times of difficulty guided all her actions, protected her from peril, and inspired her to inevitable success?

GEORGE FOX
(A.D. 1624–1691)

GEORGE FOX was indeed a Spiritualist if ever there was one. This deadly-earnest shoemaker from Leicester, in his leather suit, equipped for his revolutionary task, with will power, physical strength, a pair of magnetic eyes, and spiritual truth obtained at first hand, spent his life stumping the country, many countries, enduring persecutions, chastisements, imprisonments in the vilest of foul dens, that he might convince men of the futility of second-hand religion. And is it likely that this unlettered man would have been able to convince many thousand men and women of all classes, of the validity of his argument against second-hand religion, and have founded upon that argument a society which has already lasted for nearly three hundred years, if he himself had never had any experience of religion at first-hand?

The doctrine that he preached can be epitomized in two words, " Inward Light." By this he meant the voice of the Divine Spirit in the hearts of men, and he differed from the Churches of his day, as spiritualists of the twentieth century differ from their Churches, because instead of assuming in the " Divine Spirit " a metaphysical mystery, he gave to these words a literal interpretation. The voice —the Inward Light—spoke to him as it spoke to Socrates, and to all the great religious teachers of all times, in accents that were audible, and his one undaunted purpose in life was to bring home the fact that this Word, this Voice, is very nigh to every man, even in his heart and in his mouth.

GEORGE FOX

That this Light in very truth, "lightens every man that is born into the world." And men are hindered from listening for this voice by Sacerdotalism which teaches them to rely for grace on things external to themselves, and thus their spiritual ear becomes by disuse deaf to spiritual sound.

Fox and his first Friends were indeed called "The Children of the Light," and he ran counter to the Churches of his day because he preached that they and their followers were by their devotion to ecclesiastical forms and traditions blocking the light, and by excluding men's minds from a knowledge of the possibility of personal spiritual experience, were hindering men from a sense of their own personal relationship to God. George Fox taught Paul's doctrine that "the sons of God are those that are led by the Spirit of God," and not those who say they believe that someone else is led by the Spirit of God.

It has been well said that we cannot reckon that we have understood a truth until we find it impossible not to live in accordance with that truth. This is a hard saying, and because much discomfort is involved by living in accordance with plain truths personally revealed, people find it easier to proclaim faith in the experiences of others, and to regard as metaphysical abstractions the spiritual truths enunciated by those others. With the result that in course of time these spiritual truths become attenuated into traditions, and the experiences which occasioned the revelation of those truths, are relegated to the rubbish heap of psycho-analysis.

But for those who have themselves had opportunities of corroborating by modern experimentation the various types of experiences through which were obtained the revelations of Fox and of the great religious Teachers of the Past, it is pitiable, or ludicrous, as the mood may take you, to read the explanations afforded by most of their biographers to whom phenomena of a supernormal nature are chiefly of pathologic interest.

This is perhaps specially marked in the case of George Fox, because he, being a man of little or no worldly education, did not, like St. Teresa, offer his own commentaries and criticisms as to the character of his spiritual experiences. Anyone, however, who has even a slight knowledge of occult science will recognize in these experiences phenomena of a type which are to-day well within the realm of metapsychic experimentation.

These experiences will best be appreciated in the story of his life that is contained in his own Journal—an amazing record of physical, moral, and spiritual endurance. He was born in 1624, in the reign of James I, at a time when the history of England was in the melting-pot; but he remained singularly unconcerned as to the results of worldly battles. Whether an individual named James, or Oliver, or Charles was nominally King, had no significance for him. George Fox was the first real democrat in the history of England.

He laid the foundation in this country of the only form of democracy that could ever come within the range of practical politics. He touched the bedrock basis of democracy, for he realized that equality of privilege is only possible on the spiritual plane. But on the spiritual plane men and women of all classes and degrees can claim spiritual relationship as sons and daughters of God, as joint-heirs with Christ of the Kingdom of Heaven.

But he reached his bedrock truths, like all other seekers after truth, only after much spiritual spade-work. He was the son of a weaver, nicknamed righteous Christer, and of a mother who was an upright woman of the stock of the martyrs, and who was, says William Penn, "a woman accomplished above most of her degree in the place where she lived."

When he could barely read and write, his father apprenticed him to a shoemaker, who also dealt in wool and kept sheep and cattle. He was happiest when he was minding the sheep, for he was, even as a small boy, of a serious and religious temperament, and he found in this occupation opportunities for solitude and meditation. But one day, when he was nineteen years of age, he had been conducting some business at a fair, and one of his cousins and another

"Professor" or nominal Christian, invited him to drink beer with them at the village public house, and after they had drunk enough to quench their thirst they suggested that he who would not drink should pay all. This scandalized young Fox. He rose up, and putting his hand in his pocket, took out a groat and laid it upon the table before them, saying, "If it be so, I will leave you" (Journal).

That night he had no sleep, but he prayed and cried to the Lord in great distress that those who professed and called themselves Christians should be so unworthy of their religion. And he tells us in all simplicity that in answer to his fervent prayer the Lord spoke and told him he must forsake all, both young and old; he must keep out of all and be as a stranger unto all.

He must have been convinced of the objective nature of the command, as he forthwith left his relations and broke off all familiarity with young and old—not knowing whither it might lead.

Then, like Pythagoras, he sought spiritual counsel from those who should have been qualified to help him—from the priests. For four years he went from town to town seeking from "Professors" spiritual direction and consolation. But in vain. "The priests possessed not what they professed." And the only remedies they could suggest for his troubled soul were tobacco, dancing, psalm-singing, enlistment as a soldier, physic, blood-letting, and, as a last resource, marriage.

After four years of deep mental and spiritual distress, he realized that he must seek for himself in solitude that spiritual help which the Churches could not give. He wandered on the mountains of Yorkshire, or would sit for days in the hollow of an oak-tree, painfully searching the dark corners of his mind—which was not stocked with worldly knowledge—for some illumination.

And then began, as he terms them, his "great openings" or revelations.

One Sunday morning, as he was walking and meditating alone in the fields, he heard clairaudiently a voice which said that "to be educated at Oxford or at Cambridge was not enough to fit a man to be a minister of Christ. To teach men Hebrew, Greek, and Latin, and the seven arts . . . was not the way to make them ministers of Christ" (Bickley's *Life of Fox*).

Another day it was opened to him that God does not dwell in Temples made with hands, and he was taught that God's Church is a living entity, built up not of bricks and mortar, but of human souls, and he thenceforth calls the brick-and-mortar buildings steeple-houses, in distinction to the living assembly which is the real Church of Christ.

But the effect of these revelations was devastating to his peace of mind. For what now was there left upon which to base his religious life ? All his hopes in man were gone, there was nothing outwardly to help him, and this poor, ignorant, lonely wanderer could not tell what to do. "And then, oh then," he writes, "I heard a voice which said, 'There is one, even Christ Jesus, that can speak to thy condition.'"

A plain intimation, as it seemed to him, that the voice which now constantly adjured him was from God, and that he was being led to see that God, who was the Light of the world, and God alone, could illumine the darkness of men's hearts and cause them to acknowledge that relationship with the divine which was their birthright.

He saw that "the manifestation of the Spirit of God was given to every man to profit withal." Thus by "Inward Light," which was a manifestation of the Spirit of God, and by inward light alone could man find comfort and salvation. And all these things he saw, as he says, not by the help of man or of books, but by God's immediate Spirit and power, as did the holy men of God.

And as with these latter, the powers of evil were sometimes let loose upon him : on one occasion the natures of swine, of vipers, of Sodom and Egypt, Pharaoh, Cain, Ishmael, and Esau, etc., were shown to him by the Lord because, as he was told in answer to his cry, Why he should be thus tormented, it was needful that he should have a sense of

GEORGE FOX

all conditions—how else could he speak to all conditions? An excellent explanation this for many psychically gifted people who may have been beset by evil spirits and have been thereby discouraged.

He gives us in his Journal an exquisitely naïve account of one of his early psychic adventures, which deals, for a purpose which is soon revealed, with a question with which in that age this unlearned peasant would not have been likely in a normal way to concern himself. One morning, he says, he was sitting by the fire, and a great cloud—presumably ectoplasmic—came over him. The elements and the stars seemed all about him and a voice said, "All things come by nature,"—that is, not by the hand of God.

This seemed to him to be a temptation to deny the Deity. But he sat still and said nothing, and the people of the house perceived nothing. Then as he sat silent, a living hope arose in him and a voice which was, he says, a true voice, a real voice, said, "There is a living God who made all things." And immediately the cloud and the temptation vanished away, and life arose over it all: his heart was glad and he praised the living God.

And now follows the interesting sequel, which supplies the reason for this apparently curious revelation. Shortly after this episode, he met with people who said there was no God, but that "All things come by nature." He had a great dispute with them, and because of his revelation and because he could now speak not from supposition but from wisdom, supernormally acquired, this uncultured shoemaker overturned the arguments of his disputants and made them confess that there is a living God. Then, he says, simply, "I saw that it was good that I had gone through that exercise" (Hodgkin).

Thenceforward he conceived it his duty to impart his revelations to others, to bring them to the truth, and his great missionary work began. As might be expected, at first with an excess of zeal. For one day on his way to Nottingham, when he came to the top of a hill in sight of the town, he espied the great steeple-house, and the Lord said unto him, " Thou must go and cry against yonder great idol and against the worshippers therein."

So he went, and when he came there, " all the people looked like fallow ground, and the priest, like a great lump of earth, stood in his pulpit above." Now though quaintly enough it would have been, in accordance with custom, permissible for him as an itinerant stranger to speak or ask questions when the minister had finished, the Lord's power was so mighty and so strong upon him that he could not hold, but was made to interrupt and to cry out, " Oh, no, that is not the meaning of the text." He gave them his own views, and there was then such a disturbance that, in his own words, " The officers came and took me away and put me into a nasty stinking prison, the smell whereof got so into my nose and throat that it very much annoyed me."

The length of this imprisonment is uncertain, but after his release he again created a similar disturbance in a church at Derby, though he never again interrupted the preacher, and he was confined in a filthy dungeon for a year. But undaunted, as soon as he was free, he pursued his mission, tramped up and down the country, preaching indoors and outdoors, in season and out of season, breaking in upon courts of justice, public houses, churches, markets, fairs, and private houses, throughout England, Scotland, and Ireland, everywhere proclaiming the great principle that the value of Christianity lies not in its outer forms but in its inner, its esoteric meaning.

He therefore protested against all state establishments of religion as tending to obliterate that inner truth ; and he advocated the disuse of sacraments, tithes, a paid ministry, and set forms of prayer, and their replacement by silent worship and an unpaid ministry.

But that which aroused the greatest animosity against him and his followers was their use of the second person singular instead of the second person plural, and their refusal to take oaths or to doff hats. For this latter offence many abominable cruelties were perpetrated and many years

GEORGE FOX

of unutterable horrors in foul dungeons were endured. An example this of men's sense of proportion in matters of religion. And if spiritualists to-day feel aggrieved at the attitude towards them of the Church and of the Law, they would do well to remember the persecutions and sufferings to which Fox and his followers were subjected in their advocacy of experiential as against traditional religion.

Prisons in those days were pest-houses of inconceivable filth and horrors, and Fox spent many years within their walls. He was imprisoned at Nottingham in 1649, Derby in 1650, Carlisle 1653, London 1654, Launceston 1656, Lancaster 1660 and 1663, Scarborough for three years 1666, and Worcester for fourteen months 1674. The causes assigned were blasphemy, heresy, refusing to pay tithes, or to take an oath, the use of the second person singular, and, worst offence of all, that refusal to doff hats.

On these various counts 4,500 followers of Fox were at one time during the life of Fox, suffering the horrors of imprisonment and thirty-two died in prison (Journal).

It seems almost unnecessary again to press home the point we have so often made, but is it not clear that these men and women, whose confidence in their Leader was strong enough to enable them to endure hardships and cruelties almost inconceivable to-day, would not have had that confidence in the teaching of the shoemaker, if he had merely preached to them of a far-away, historic Christ? They were enabled to endure because the Christ of whom he spoke was a living Christ, an indwelling Spirit, who not only was to each one of them an Inward Light illuminating all their path, but He manifested His Presence and His power by signs and wonders which no one could dispute.

By these signs and wonders which Fox wrought, his disciples perceived that he spoke that which he knew, and testified to that which he had seen. In other words, Fox had considerable psychic powers. He cured disease: he was clairvoyant: he was a discerner of spirits, and could exorcise evil spirits: he foretold coming events. For instance, a fortnight before Oliver Cromwell broke up the

Long Parliament—the Rump—he prophesied, or had "an opening" from the Lord, that before that day two weeks, the Parliament would be dissolved and the Speaker plucked out of his chair."

Whilst in prison in Scarborough he had "a Divine warning" of the Great Fire of London which broke out the day after his release. He was given a sight beforehand of the revolution of 1688. A great weight came upon him and the Lord gave him a sight of the great bustles and troubles, revolution and change, which soon after came to pass.

Once he was entranced for fourteen days, when he lay, his whole person transformed, and he was then incapable of being bled.

He had experiences, too, which were beyond the range of the average medium, experiences similar to those of Pythagoras, of Swedenborg, and of Jacob Boehme. For instance, during a trance, the whole of creation was "opened" to him, and he saw into the natures, into the essences of all things (Journal). And so realistic was the vision thus vouchsafed that he wondered afterwards whether, as he now knew the natures and virtues of things, he ought not to practise physic for the good of mankind.

On another occasion the Lord "opened" to him "things relating to those three great professions, Law, Physic, and Divinity (so-called)"; and he was shown that the lawyers, the doctors, and the clergy, by not knowing the inner natures and principles and essences of things, made rulings which were not after the wisdom, the equity, or the spirit of God.

His disciples also had psychic gifts, and signs and wonders accompanied their teaching. They practised exorcism, prophecy, and clairvoyance; they healed the sick: had visions and heard voices: and generally exercised the apostolic gifts, though Fox himself regarded such signs and wonders as incidental to his mission.

The psychic power at some of those first enthusiastic Meetings of the Friends must have been tremendous. The whole house in which they sat would shake, and on one occasion a clergyman present was so terrified that he ran out of the church lest it should fall upon him.

At Fox's preaching the people fell in trances, swoons, and ecstasies, and foamed at the mouth as they did in Acts x. 44, Dan. x. 9, Hab. iii. 16, Isa. lxvi. 5, Joel ii. 6.

In October 1669, at the age of forty-five, when he was abnormally aged by his persecutions and imprisonments. he married the widow of a Cumberland Judge, Margaret Fell, who had been for years his noble friend and fellow-martyr in the Cause. But neither he nor she had much time to devote to such trivialities, and though devoted to each other, within a week of their marriage they parted, "betaking themselves to their several services," she to prison from March 1670 to April 1671, and it was shortly after her release that in the spring of 1671 Fox sailed for America and the West Indies to visit the Friends who had settled in Maryland and in Rhode Island in order to benefit from the religious toleration which there prevailed, though Massachusetts was, on the contrary, a scene of the grossest bigotry, and four Quaker martyrs, three men and one woman, were all hung at Boston for no other offence than that of being Friends (Hodgkin).

Only later, when his health was much broken, did he enjoy any pause in his incessant journeyings, and then twice, two years at a time, he and his wife—the mother of a large family and nine years older than himself—enjoyed the happiness of a home life at her beautiful house, Swarthmore Hall, in the country of the Lakes.

But at such times he busied himself with his pen, writing books and epistles, and with the affairs of the ever-growing Society of Friends.

In 1677 he had paid a short visit to the Continent, with William Penn and Robert Barclay, to encourage Friends in Holland and in Germany, and this visit was repeated in 1684. In the interval his time was chiefly spent in London and the suburbs, and the home counties, that he might the better look after Friends' sufferings under the persecutions due to the Conventicle Act.

These were only lessened in 1687 by the Declaration of Indulgence. It was four years later, in 1691, that he was finally released from the imprisonment of the flesh and obtained that freedom which is mis-named death, but which is, as we believe, the gateway to eternal life.

And in estimating the value of Fox's influence on the religious history of the world, we must not seek for originality. There is no such thing as originality in religion, except in the sense that all true religion is, as Fox intimated, original in the heart of man. The work of a religious teacher who is a genius in religion is not to found a new cult—nothing was ever further from Fox's thoughts—but to show man that to fit himself to receive the Divine imprint, he must first make clean the tablet of his soul; he must apply the sponge and obliterate the vain scribblings of Sacerdotalism, and so leave *tabula rasa* for the Finger of God.

There were in Fox's day many dissenting sects: Presbyterians, Independents, Seekers, Baptists, Episcopal Men, Socinians, Brownists, Lutherans, Calvinists, Arminians, Fifth-Monarchy Men, Familists, Muggletonians, and Ranters. All these were struggling in their various ways after the same Inward Light. And Fox's contribution to religious thought was that he centralized, he focussed to a single point the Idea which incoherently they were all trying to express, the Idea for which the Age was ripe: he gathered the threads frayed from these various faiths and wove them into a spiritual garment that could be worn by all men.

Fox tells us that none of these others dared to affirm that they had the same power and Spirit that the Apostles had and were in; and it was in his acknowledgment of this Divine Power and Spirit that he, Fox, was given by the Lord dominion over them all (Journal).

Even those who may differ from the views of this great Friend of man, would probably agree with Carlyle when he says: " No grander thing was ever done than when George Fox, stitching himself a suit of leather, went forth, determined to find truth for himself and to do battle for it against all superstition, bigotry, and intolerance."

And can we suppose that this son of a poor weaver would have gone forth and have faced the most appalling persecutions both for himself and his followers, if he had merely been re-stating traditions concerning experiences of 1900 years ago—if he had been, like the clergy of the established Churches, merely, as it were, editing those remote experiences.

It was with Fox as with all our other examples: He had power as a teacher of religion because he taught not what he had learnt from others who had themselves learnt from books and from traditions, but because he spoke from personal experience of the reality of spirit and of the possibility of communion with the world beyond. It was because he had personal experience of the truths that he expounded and because he lived as though he knew that what he said was true, that George Fox became a dynamic force in the religions of the world.

SWEDENBORG

(A.D. 1688–1772)

SWEDENBORG has been called the greatest spiritualistic medium that ever lived, possibly because those who so speak are not conversant with the history of the other great Initiates who preceded him, and whose occult powers we have here outlined. But he was a giant amongst mediums. He was a man, too, who would have been of invaluable service to the cause of psychic science to-day, for he would not have been content to be a member of a psychical research society which fills lumber rooms with evidence of the veridity of spirit happenings, but which makes scanty use of the evidence as a stepping-stone to further knowledge.

His inventive genius and his scientific mind would have busied themselves in devising in laboratories means of probing the multifarious and baffling phenomena of our modern séance rooms.

Unfortunately, however, for the world, Swedenborg lived in an age that was intermediate between the good old days when a knowledge of cosmic truths was regarded as a sacred heritage—too sacred to be broadcasted to the multitude—and the now dawning day when this knowledge is being handled in scientific laboratories, and he spent the first fifty years of his life in the vain hope that he would discover the nature and the seat of the Soul of man, by a study of the anatomy of man, when he might as well have hoped to discover the nature of a butterfly by a study of its cocoon.

His great works bearing upon this subject were *The*

Economy of the Animal Kingdom, considered Anatomically, Physically, and Philosophically, described by Emerson (Representative Men) as "one of those books which by the sustained dignity of thinking is an honour to the human race." And *The Animal Kingdom,* which Emerson considers to be "a book of wonderful merits."

From his earliest childhood Swedenborg had a hankering after spiritual things. His parents said that as a small boy "angels spoke through his mouth," and though at first sight it seems tragical that his marvellously inventive, scientific, and capacious brain should for so many years have led him on a false quest, Providence was in charge, and discreetly ordained that his reputation as one of the greatest and sanest scientists of the day should be firmly established before the noise of his marvellous psychic experiences should be bruited abroad.

For it would not be easy to condemn as a half-witted charlatan, or as an hysterical fool, or to treat with anything but respect the beliefs and assertions of a man whose scientific reputation was second to none in Europe.

He foreshadowed the nebular hypothesis twenty-one years before Kant and sixty-two years before Laplace. He realized the motor centres in the brain before this was corroborated by the German and English physiologists. He is said to have discovered the atomic theory, the undulatory theory of light: that heat is a mode of motion: that magnetism and electricity are forms of ethereal motion; that molecular forces are due to the action of an ethereal medium.

He was a mathematician, philosopher, physiologist, chemist, engineer, mineralogist, anatomist, astronomer, geologist, psychologist, poet and musician, and in all these subjects he made brilliant scientific discoveries.

Incidentally he was practised in various handicrafts such as book-binding, engraving, lens grinding, manufacture of mathematical instruments, etc. He invented also, amongst many other things, a flying machine, a submarine war vessel, a quick-firing gun, and a mercurial air-pump. As Emerson says of him, "He led the most real life of any man then in the world." He was therefore not the kind of man to be deceived by mental illusions. On the contrary, like St. Teresa, he criticized all his experiences with scientific eye, to guard himself from snares of phantasy and imagination.

When, therefore, a man of this calibre asserted that he was on intimate terms with spirits who spoke to him " as one man speaks to another," and when, moreover, the examples of his psychic powers with which he astonished Europe were admittedly only explicable on a spiritistic hypothesis, the cause of Spiritualism was exalted to a stage beyond that to which it had sunk in those materialistic days.

But in estimating the evidential value of Swedenborg's seership, it is helpful to take into account not only his intellectual but his moral qualities, and these were of such a nature as to prohibit the possibility of any inclusion of fraud or chicanery.

Trobridge devotes a whole chapter to the testimonies written of him by distinguished people, who were his contemporaries, and there is, as he says, but one voice, that of unqualified praise, even from those who disagree entirely with his views. " He was a pattern of virtue and of reverence for his Maker, for in him there was no sort of double dealing." " We cannot discover in him any sign of arrogance, rashness, or intention to deceive." " He was a pattern of sincerity, virtue, and piety, and at the same time the most learned man in the kingdom." " He was righteous, just, and a most learned man." All, indeed, from the highest to the lowest, of those who passed judgment are unanimous in testifying not only to his learning but to his high moral character and his general reliability. We cannot, therefore, lightly relegate the occurrence of supernormal phenomena either to illusion or to fraud.

Swedenborg was born in Stockholm in 1688, during the reign of Charles XII, who frequently consulted and honoured him. He was the son of a Swedish bishop in West Jutland, who himself believed in direct inspiration from the spirit-world. Indeed, the name he gave this son must have been an inspiration, for he called him "Emanuel"—God with us—that he might, he said, be constantly reminded of the nearness of God. Swedenborg was thus fortunate in having been brought up in a sympathetically spiritual atmosphere.

He received a liberal education, and after his University course at Upsala, he followed the fashion of all our great Initiates and travelled in foreign lands. He visited the universities of England, Holland, France, and Germany, and he journeyed over Europe examining mines and smelting works, always, however, deeply studying all the natural sciences upon the afore-mentioned supposition that with the scalpel of the physicist he would one day be able to dissect the soul.

But at the age of fifty-six years, when presumably he had learnt as much of worldly science as was deemed necessary by the higher powers, a change came over him. He had all his life enjoyed extraordinary visions, and heard voices, and seen lights, but now he received a direct revelation and command, as he believed from the Lord.

A spirit appeared to him on two successive nights, and on the second night "a certain spirit" spoke and told him that he had been chosen to unfold to men the spiritual sense of the Holy Scripture. "I will myself dictate," said the spirit, "what thou shalt write."

That same night the world of spirits—hell and heaven—was convincingly opened to him, and from that time forth, he gave up all worldly learning and earthly ambition, and laboured only in spiritual things according as the Lord commanded him. Thereafter, he says, the Lord daily opened the eyes of his soul, to see in perfect wakefulness what was going on in the other world and to converse, wide awake, with angels and spirits.

From this moment, he realized that neither geometrical nor physical, nor metaphysical principles alone would enable him to grasp the true nature of soul and spirit, or the relation of the finite to the infinite; this could only be perceived by spiritual insight. And it is interesting to notice that one of the main principles which was in this manner revealed to Swedenborg was the doctrine of what he calls " Universal Correspondency "—a doctrine analogous to Plato's doctrine of " Ideas," which Plato derived, as we have seen, through Socrates from Pythagoras ; the doctrine, namely, that things material are a manifestation of things spiritual : the belief that everything outward and visible has an inward and spiritual cause : the doctrine of St. Paul, who says, " the invisible things of Him from the creation of the world are clearly seen, being understood by the things that are made " (Rom. i. 20).

As this is a belief which is still held by the best and wisest men to-day, we thus see once more that in the main all revelations teach the same great basic truths, though these truths may be variously garbed in accordance with the differing requirements of the Ages.

Swedenborg now resigned the post which he had held as Assessor at the Board of Mines, and gave himself up to the work for which he had been commissioned, because, he said, " spirits cannot speak with a man who is much devoted to worldly and corporeal cares." But he never for a moment regretted the years spent in scientific research on the physical plane : he understood that this study had been necessary in order that spiritual truths might be presented by the light of science, to satisfy reason as well as heart.

His great work, *Arcana Cœlestia*, is an exposition, as commanded by the Lord, of the spiritual sense of Genesis and of Exodus : and it attributes occult meaning to that which is in the Bible otherwise incomprehensible. It comprised eight volumes, containing 10,837 paragraphs, which were, he claimed, derived by direct illumination from the Lord.

Indeed, his life now was spent more with angels than with men : he was in the world, but not of it : though, when not in trance, he was always ready to welcome visitors who desired to hear his teaching or to catch glimpses of some marvel. He always, however, sternly refused to use his power of communication with the other world for the purpose of merely gratifying the vulgar or sentimental curiosity of would-be sitters, or for any but the most cogent reasons. He refused to pander to the commercial desire to regain lost articles or to discover hidden treasures. He refused, in short, to prostitute a great gift to unworthy ends.

Of his psychic powers the most documentative proofs are afforded by three well-known stories. On a certain occasion the Queen of Sweden, wife of Adolphus Frederick, a woman who was, as she herself confessed, not easily duped, asked Swedenborg, half in jest, if he had seen her brother, Frederick the Great of Prussia, who had lately passed over? Swedenborg said, "No," he had not. "Well, if you should see him," replied the Queen, "remember me to him." Eight days later, Swedenborg again came to Court, but early, before the Queen had left her apartment in which she was talking with her maids of honour.

Without, however, waiting for the Queen to come out, Swedenborg went straight into her room, and whispered in her ear. The Queen, struck dumb with astonishment at what she heard, was taken ill and did not recover herself for some minutes. When she came to herself, Swedenborg had left, and she said to those about her, "There is only God and my brother who can know what that man has just told me." She owned that Swedenborg had reminded her of her last correspondence with the Prince, the subject of which was known to themselves alone.

An amusing story illustrative of the way in which Swedenborg lived in two worlds at one and the same time, is told by the poet Atterbom in a book published in 1841. He tells how as a graduate from the University, he was on his travels, and arrived at Stockholm. Here he felt it a duty to visit the renowned and wonderful old Seer. On reaching the house he was shown into the parlour by a good-natured old servant, who then went into an inner apartment to announce him to Swedenborg. The servant returned immediately with an apology from her master, who had said he was engaged with another visitor, but that the latter would soon be leaving.

The poet was requested to take a seat and was left alone in the parlour. Now his chair chanced to be near the door of the inner room, and he could not help hearing that a lively conversation was going on, while someone walked up and down the room. He could hear every word that was said, and as the conversation was in Latin and concerned the antiquities of Rome, in which the poet was specially interested, he listened with the deepest attention.

But he was puzzled because he only heard one voice speaking, between pauses of silence which seemed to convey answers that entirely satisfied the one who spoke. Atterbom assumed that the voice belonged to Swedenborg, who seemed to be highly pleased with his guest.

Suddenly the door opened, and Swedenborg, who was of course recognizable from his public portraits, came out into the parlour, his face beaming with joy. He nodded casually to Atterbom, who had risen from his seat, and with his attention apparently fixed upon someone who was invisible to the poet, he ushered this invisible someone to the door and in fluent Latin phrases begged for an early repetition of the visit.

Swedenborg then turned back to Atterbom and, apologizing, said: "I had, as you will have observed, a visitor. Can you guess who it was?" "No, impossible," replied the amazed poet. "My dear Sir," said Swedenborg, "only think—it was Virgil—a fine and pleasant fellow. I always had a good opinion of the man, and he deserves it. He is modest as he is witty, and most agreeably entertaining."

The poet afterwards visited Swedenborg several times, and he confesses that he never perceived the least that was extraordinary excepting only his amazing learning in all the branches of human science. He only regretted that on a certain point, a screw in the venerable man was loose, or altogether fallen away.

But perhaps the most widely discussed of Swedenborg's psychic adventures is the story of the fire at Stockholm. For this was carefully investigated by the philosopher

Kant, who thereafter, in a letter to Charlotte Knobloch, dated Königsberg, August 10, 1758, acknowledges that "the following occurrence appears to me to have the greatest weight of proof, and to place the assertion respecting Swedenborg's extraordinary gift beyond all possibility of doubt."

Kant then tells the story of how in the year 1759, on a Saturday, towards the end of September, Swedenborg arrived about 4 p.m. at Gothenburg from England (which was his second home, from which many of his books were published), and was invited with a party of fifteen other people to the house of a friend. At 6 p.m. he went out, and after a short interval returned looking pale and alarmed. He said that at the Södermalm in Stockholm, which was about 300 miles from Gothenburg, a dangerous fire had just broken out, and that it was spreading very fast. He was restless and went out often; and he reported that the house of one of his friends, whom he named, was already in ashes, and that his own was in danger. At 8 p.m. he joyfully exclaimed, "Thank God, the fire is extinguished the third door from my house."

The news occasioned great commotion throughout the city and it was announced to the Governor the same evening. On Sunday morning Swedenborg was summoned to the Governor, who questioned him concerning the disaster. Swedenborg described the fire precisely, how it had begun, and in what manner it had ceased, and how long it had continued.

On Monday evening a messenger arrived at Gothenburg, who was despatched by the Board of Trade during the time of the fire. In the letters brought by him the fire was described precisely in the manner stated by Swedenborg. "On Tuesday morning the Royal Courier arrived at the Governor's with the melancholy intelligence of the fire, of the loss which it had occasioned, and of the houses it had damaged and ruined, not in the least differing from that which Swedenborg had given at the very time when it happened; for the fire was extinguished at eight o'clock." [1]

[1] *Life of Emanuel Swedenborg*, by G. Trobridge, pp. 223-24.

But Kant, in another letter to his friend, Charlotte von Knobloch, to whom we should be grateful, gives an account of an incident which had been carefully investigated and corroborated in every detail by a friend upon the spot. The story concerned a Madame Harteville, widow of the Dutch Ambassador in Stockholm. "She had been called upon," writes Kant, "by a goldsmith to pay for a silver service which her husband had purchased. But feeling certain that her husband would not have neglected to pay the debt, and because the amount was considerable, she requested Swedenborg to have the kindness to ask her husband how it was with the silver service. Swedenborg consented, and three days later he called at her house, and in his cool way told her that he had conversed with her husband, that the debt had been paid seven months before his decease, and that the receipt was in a bureau in the room upstairs.

"Madame, who had company in the drawing-room for coffee, replied that the bureau had been quite cleared out, and that the receipt had not been amongst the papers. But Swedenborg said that her husband had described to him how after pulling out the left-hand drawer a board would appear, which required to be drawn out, when a secret compartment would be disclosed containing his private Dutch correspondence, as well as the receipt.

"Upon hearing this description, the whole company rose and accompanied the lady into the room upstairs. The bureau was opened : they did as they were directed : the compartment was found, of which no one had ever known before : and to the great astonishment of all, the papers were discovered there, in accordance with his description."

It seems that Madame von Knobloch, not knowing what to believe, concerning the seership of Swedenborg, had asked Kant to give her his judgment on the matter, and to oblige her, Kant had instituted searching inquiries into the occurrences, with the result that is embodied in these letters (Trobridge).

But Kant was, and naturally, nervous lest his friends

should think he had shown too much credulity, and he adds that he is not aware that anybody has ever perceived in him an inclination to the marvellous, or a weakness tending to credulity, but that in all the narratives of apparitions and of visions concerning the spiritual world which had been known to him he had always considered it to be most in agreement with the rule of sound reason to incline to the negative side, not that he imagined such things to be impossible, but because the instances were in general not well proved (Wilkinson) . . . until the report concerning Swedenborg came to his notice.

He had then caused stringent inquiries to be set on foot, and finally Kant, after narrating the stories of the fire, etc., concludes with these words: " What can be brought forward against the authenticity of these occurrences ? " This authenticity evidently surprised Kant, as he explains how " in order not to reject blindfold the prejudice against apparitions and visions by a new prejudice, I found it desirable to inform myself of the particulars of the transactions " —an example which might well be followed by philosophers to-day.

But now, as a constant visitor to the spirit-world, what sort of picture of it does Swedenborg paint for us ? He gives us a point of view which differs absolutely from that held by the orthodox Churches of to-day, but it is a view which in its general outlines is corroborated by modern seers and by those who have held intercourse with spirits on the plane beyond.

He tells us, for instance, that the next world is not a heaven of languorous ease but of interesting activities. Education, art, music, literature, architecture, science, are earnestly pursued ; even embroidery and knitting are not despised. Men and women live as men and women after death, and they take with them to an intermediate state, where souls are prepared for final abode, their powers and capacities, their beliefs and prejudices.

The spirit-world, indeed, is this same old familiar world of ours, " the same old world of God " continued in a higher sphere. Everything with which we are familiar here is perpetuated there. And if it be true that material objects are manifestations of spiritual things, then this perpetuation is an understandable fact. Therefore, all that we learn here is not thrown away, but forms the basis of a higher knowledge. " Thus friendships with flowers, birds, rivers, animals, sea and sky, will never be dissolved."

And thus it comes well within the range of possibility that belief even in Raymond Lodge's much-discussed spirit cigar would for Swedenborg present no intellectual difficulty. Indeed the more we learn of psychic science the more we realize how guarded it behoves us to be in our criticisms of the experiences of those endowed with fourth-dimensional consciousness. " It is very singular, or at least very remarkable," wrote the Abbé Pernetz, " that almost all those who have read the writings of Swedenborg for the purpose of refuting them, have finished by adopting his views." And similarly, there are to-day many who have set out to study spiritualism in order to confute it, who have been compelled in honesty to enter the spiritualist fold.

But indeed it ought by now to be easy to deal with the difficulties of honest sceptics, for the same questions are always posed, and to these questions classical answers have been supplied. A question, for instance, that is frequently asked is : Why if some men have this psychic faculty, is it not possessed by all men ? And this is the answer given by Swedenborg when asked by some friends how it was that he seemed to have the monopoly of talking with lofty persons in the higher spheres : " Every man," he replied, " might at the present day have this faculty as well as in the times of the Old Testament ; but that the true hindrance was the sensual state into which mankind had fallen."

He further added that : " As Man is at present constituted, it would be dangerous if there were universal communication with spirits. For as we are all in association with our likes we, being full of evil, would attract evil spirits, who would but confirm us in our evil ways, and lend to those ways an authority from which it would be hard to escape."

He then confessed that even he himself, whenever he was intent upon worldly affairs, or was absorbed in money matters, lapsed into a bodily state, and that then the spirits, as they informed him, could not speak, as "their ideas became, as it were, drowned within his body."

Swedenborg, who correctly foretold the day of his death, died in his beloved London in 1772, at the age of eighty-four. And in looking back dispassionately at his genius and at his great psychic, moral, and spiritual qualities, it would seem at first sight that his influence in the world has been incommensurate with his qualities. For though during his lifetime he was held in high repute as a learned and spiritual wonder, and after his death a Church—the new Church— was founded, and he has to-day many thousands of followers both in this country and in Europe and in the United States, yet to the majority of people to-day Swedenborg is only known by name—as a psychic freak, who spent half his life in supposed intercourse with angels. Only the few have troubled to compare the experiences of this great intellectual Seer with the experiences of both ancient and modern seekers after spiritual truth, and are thus able to realize that in a time of great materialistic darkness Swedenborg was in his right place in that chain of great Initiates who are commissioned to pass on the illuminating Torch of Truth.

God's ways are not our ways, and it is sometimes ordained that streams of living water shall for a time flow underground to emerge into the sunshine when conditions for their fructifying services shall be appropriate; but in the meantime they never cease to exercise an influence. And it would seem that whether acknowledged or unacknowledged Swedenborg's teaching permeated many of the great minds whose opinions we to-day respect.

Trobridge suggests that Tennyson, the Brownings, Coventry Patmore, Ruskin, George MacDonald, Henry Drummond, Oliver Wendell Holmes, Thoreau, Elizabeth Stuart Phelps, Goethe, Heine, Balzac, Coleridge, and

Emerson were all more or less tinctured with his ideas, whilst Carlyle's *Sartor Resartus* is saturated with Swedenborg.

And we may, I think, assume, that the value of Swedenborg as a religious teacher will in the future be appreciated more and more, and according to the degree in which those who study spiritualism desire not merely to find their friends, but to find God.

And to those who deem it an insanity to believe with Swedenborg that intercourse with angels—with holy spirits—is within the compass of man's powers, we would suggest that it might be better to be mad with Swedenborg than sane with the Bolshevistic and un-Christian Lenin.

JOHN WESLEY
(1703-1791)

JOHN WESLEY stands in a slightly different category to the religious teachers whom we have hitherto discussed, for though he was a brilliant example of the influence of psychic phenomena upon religious life, his "conversion," the initiatory factor in his life's work, had not the objective character which has in our other examples been conspicuous. His "conversion" in that little city room in Aldersgate Street, one of the most fateful events of a fateful century, "an event that was pregnant with the fate of Protestantism," was not accompanied by outward and visible signs, it was an inspiration which fell silently, as dew from Heaven, upon a soul that had for years been parched and barren, thirsting for a sign from God.

Psychic manifestations of the objective order followed immediately upon his first inspiration, and served as proofs of his heaven-sent mission, but the determining revelation came silently, as a thief in the night, at a prosaic moment whilst he was listening to a dull reading, a translation of Luther's preface to the Epistle to the Romans. It came without form or substance as a message in the language of Heaven, which is ideas not words.

He became suddenly aware that God was present, and was branding on his soul a great truth—so simple that it had hitherto escaped him—the truth, namely, that sin and death can have no power over the soul that is "made in the image of God." And immediately the pettifogging sins which had troubled his conscience, and the intellectual doubts which had disturbed his religious peace of mind, dissolved like gossamer in the morning sunshine, under the glow of a divine radiance which warmed his heart, assured him of divine grace, and revolutionized his life; for he realized that this was a revelation, a tidings of great joy which must be broadcasted to the world.

For thirteen years, ever since his ordination, until this great moment, he had been stumbling and struggling along dark paths beset with theological and casuistical obstacles. As a scholar and a Fellow of Lincoln College, Oxford, he had made a deep study of theology, and in the hope of obtaining assurance of the grace of God, he had worn himself out in self-sacrificing works of piety, charity, and asceticism.

But all in vain. His religious life had so far been a failure. It had brought no peace of mind to himself nor any benefit to others. For two years, from 1727 to 1729, he had officiated as curate to his father at Epworth and at Wroote, but though he possessed endowments which would seem to have qualified him for an exceptional degree of success— he was not only a scholar, he was of good birth, a fine speaker, he had a tireless enthusiasm, and an austere conception of religious duty—yet he failed. "I preached much," he says, "but saw no fruit of my labour. . . . For how indeed," he asks, "could it be otherwise, when I took it for granted that all to whom I preached were believers?"

He failed also egregiously as a missionary in Georgia and Savannah. Having returned from Epworth to Oxford, where he spent six years in religious drudgery, he went to Georgia in 1735, to convert the American Indians, and to minister to the settlers. But amongst the Indians he found no one who wanted to be converted, and with the settlers he was so tactless and injudicious, working on the narrow ecclesiastical plane, amongst people who craved above all things liberty of thought and action, that he was arraigned for technical church misdemeanours, before a grand jury of forty-four persons, and was driven out of

JOHN WESLEY

the Colony after a miserable experience of two years and four months. As he later realized, he had hoped to convert others before he himself was converted

But if he had already been, for all these years, a devout Christian, what was the nature of this conversion which came to Wesley in that Aldersgate Street room ? Coleridge, in his editorial notes on Southey's *Life of Wesley*, considers that the " assurance " which came to Wesley " amounted to little more than a strong pulse or throb of sensibility, accompanying the vehement volition of acquiescence, an ardent desire to find the position true, and a concurring determination to receive it as true."

And in the similar case of John's brother, Charles, Coleridge attributes his conversion to " an inrush feeling of convalescence after pleurisy, which taking its shape and colour from the predominating thoughts and images, becomes assurance and efficient faith."

And in cases where pleurisy could not be assigned as the contributory cause, the place of the pleurisy is, says Coleridge, supplied by " the disease produced by the mental disturbance itself of the passionate straining after the new birth."

If Coleridge's estimate of the nature of the phenomena which transformed both Charles and John Wesley, and was the initiatory cause of the redemption from vice, from irreligion, from the dead formalism of ecclesiasticism, of many thousands of people scattered over three great continents—if this was, indeed, all due to pleuritic causes, there is no need to seek further for proofs of miracles of a truly supernatural kind.

But may we not more reasonably accept the hypothesis that Wesley, like all his great predecessors who became teachers of religion, received during those blessed moments of inspiration such assurance of the reality of the spirit-world that thenceforth he could not fail to speak with conviction of that world ? That he realized during that revelation, not only that there is indeed a Kingdom of Heaven, but that this Kingdom is within us : that Wesley, in short, through the whispering of a Holy Spirit, learned once and for ever the great secret of Pentecost?

He had been a long time learning it, and we cannot but believe that he never would have learnt it, for his mind had worked along purely moral and intellectual lines, if it had not been for an early influence which consciously or unconsciously must, when the time was ripe, have given objective reality to his belief in the spirit-world—the influence, namely, of those weird spiritualistic occurrences which took place in his father's Rectory at Epworth, whilst he was a boy, a schoolboy at the Charterhouse.

Therefore, though these psychic occurrences were not of a very elevating type, it is worth while briefly to consider them as the humble antecedents of later and more transcendental spiritual experiences. Also the phenomena were so well authenticated that the story of Old Jeffry, as the Wesley girls called the unseen operator, constitutes, as Fitchett says, one of the best attested ghost stories in literature.

The occurrences which disturbed the peace of the Rector's family circle for about four months, from December 1716 to April 1717, were of the Poltergeist type—noises of all kinds, knockings here, there, and everywhere, groanings, clattering as of smashed bottles, gobblings as of a turkey-cock, steps up and down stairs at all hours of the day and night, etc.: all mischievous, but not malicious.

"Old Jeffry" was evidently something of a gentleman, for when he was on duty he would lift the latches of the doors, as the girls came near to pass through; and when Mrs. Wesley appealed to him not to disturb her between the hours of 5 to 6 p.m., and requested that he would keep quiet whilst she was at her devotions, Old Jeffry unfailingly respected her wishes.[1]

This disturber of the peace was also evidently an ardent Jacobite; he would kick the floor, or the walls, with boisterous energy whenever the Rector prayed for King George I. And on those occasions, John's father, determined not to

---

[1] *Wesley and his Century*, by Fitchett.

be suppressed by a mere ghost, would repeat the prayer in yet more defiant tones.

Indeed, it seems not impossible that Old Jeffry may in his clumsy way have been trying to punish the Rector for his political intolerance towards his wife. For one day, this arrogant little lord and master, noticing that Mrs. Wesley did not join in the Amen to the prayer for the Dutch King William, had demanded an explanation, and when she confessed that her true king lived over the water, and when moreover she refused to recant, he became fiercely indignant at this sign of political independence on the part of a mere female, and so making up by arrogance what he evidently lacked in humour, he announced grandiloquently : " Sukie ! If we are to have two kings, we must have two beds." And without more ado, the irascible and irresponsible little god took horse and rode away, leaving his parish and a considerable number of their nineteen children for many months to the care of his brilliantly clever, cultured, and practical wife. If, therefore, Old Jeffry had in mind to chasten the Rector's marital arrogance, he has our sympathy.

Now John Wesley believed implicitly with everybody else that the occurrences were of an objective nature, and in the article which he published in the *Arminian Magazine*, describing the events, he affords a clue, interesting to students of similar phenomena, to the possible mediumistic centre of the disturbances. He mentions during the course of his narrative, that one evening when his father and the vicar of a neighbouring village—an eminently pious and sensible man—were trying to locate the phenomena, they followed the knockings into the nursery, where two of the smaller children and his sister Hetty were lying asleep, and they found these children " though asleep, sweating and trembling exceedingly." Here, therefore, doubtless, was the mediumistic focussing point of these manifestations.

Indeed, Hetty would to-day be singled out by investigators of such-like occurrences as the chief mediumistic force used by Old Jeffry, for we read in a letter written by Emily Wesley to her brother Samuel that she, Emily, was "not much frighted at first and very little at last; but it was never near me, except two or three times, and never followed me *as it did my sister Hetty*. I have been with her when it has knocked under her, and when she has removed, has followed, and still kept just under her feet, which was enough to terrify a stouter person."

But our present object is not to explain the phenomena or to prove their validity, but to record the fact that they were accepted by the whole Wesley family as indubitable communications from the spirit-world. They knew nothing in those days of psychic rods, or of ectoplasmic exudations, and they had to content themselves with the philosophy expressed in Samuel Wesley's epigram: " Wit," he said, " might find many explanations of the phenomena, but Wisdom none." Surely a wiser sentiment than that of Coleridge, who attributed the occurrences to " a contagious disease, to the auditual nerves, what vapours or blue devils are to the eye."

But the phenomena, even though inexplicable, must have deeply impressed—amongst the rest—the schoolboy, John Wesley, with a sense of the reality and of the objective nearness of the other world.

Emily Wesley, in a letter to her brother Samuel, telling him of the latest performances of Old Jeffry, testifies to the religious effect produced upon herself. " I am so far," she writes, " from being superstitious that I was too much inclined to infidelity, so that I heartily rejoiced at having such an opportunity of convincing myself, past doubt or scruple, of the existence of some beings besides those we see" (Southey).

And John, thus in early days convinced of the reality behind the religion in which he had been in Spartan fashion brought up by his wonderful mother, had within him a foundation which would later give concrete reality to the mysteries of spirit inspiration, even when, as at his conversion, the spirit was itself invisible to human eye.

Indeed, Emily's remark is in itself justification for the study of psychic phenomena of the physical order. They are a means to an end, and these Epworth happenings, which left no room for doubt in the minds of the Wesley family as to their supernormal origin, must undoubtedly have served as solid base for John's subsequent belief in the possibility of spirit—of divine intervention.

Thus the influence of those early crude, but objective experiences, enabled him to understand that the whispering of the Spirit in that dingy room in Aldersgate Street, proceeded not from a mere ecclesiastical and metaphysical abstraction called " the Holy Ghost," but from a real, live, sympathetic Holy Spirit.

But as Wesley's new birth was only effected after years of severe travailing, he might never have come to the birth, or he might have been stillborn, stifled by his own futile intellectual strugglings, had not the Moravian Missionary, Peter Bohler, in timely fashion served as midwife to his soul. He it was who brought his soul from darkness into light by showing him that assurance of grace and of divine love, " conversion " as it was called, must be the result not of outward works or of theological creeds, or of lifeless ritual, but of personal revelation.

Wesley had, like many, made the mistake of supposing that prayer, fasting, church-going, charity, virtue, asceticism, were themselves religion or the causes of religion, whereas, as he now learnt, these were only the effects of a religious state of mind which itself could only be brought about by personal experience of a different order. These acts of piety, etc., had become confounded with religion because they almost invariably followed as the result of religious experience; but though they might predispose to the condition of mind essential for the reception of religious experience, the latter has its source elsewhere.

Hitherto he had believed that divinely given consciousness of acceptance by God was only granted occasionally to great Saints, and it was in this discovery of the possibility of personal revelation for every child of man that lay the whole secret of the power and influence of Wesley, not only as a reformer, but as the founder of what was in the end, practically a new Church.

For years Wesley, though leading mechanically the life of a Saint, and though intellectually, morally, and ecclesiastically a model of religion, had been unhappy and unsatisfied. In spite of all his virtuous deeds, once when his life was in danger during a storm at sea, he had trembled and asked himself, " What if the Gospel be not true ? " His soul had starved on unilluminated theology and tyrannical tradition.

Once in Georgia he was tortured with remorse at the crime of having baptized an Indian child with only two sponsors instead of the authorized three, and so tenacious was he of ecclesiastical custom that he would, as he acknowledged, have thought saving of souls to be almost a sin if not done inside a church.

No one, therefore, could have been better qualified than Wesley to appraise the relative value of a religion based on traditions of the past and on the revelations of others, and a religion based upon present-day and personal revelations. And Wesley stood defiantly and whole-heartedly for the soul-stirring religion of personal revelation as against the ecclesiastical traditions of a supine Church. He reaffirmed and restated the same old truth which has been stressed throughout these pages, that knowledge of spiritual facts can only be acquired through spiritual channels. He asserted with passionate conviction, because he knew from personal experience what he was talking about, that a mere academic affirmation of belief in God, in Christ, and in religion, even though accompanied by the virtues of a thousand saints, would not bring assurance—assurance of the Grace of God, of the reality of Spirit. Man must have an inner, a personal experience before he could call himself religious or consider that he had found God.

Therefore, though to Anglicans it may seem that the Wesleyan Methodism of to-day is a somewhat dreary and

JOHN WESLEY

soulless institution, we must look beyond the inappropriate name of Methodism, beyond the architecturally ugly conventicles in which the Wesleyans often worship, we must look back to the life of the founder, and find in his inspiration the driving force which made thieves honest, drunkards sober, and harlots chaste, and which opened the hearts of eighteenth-century unbelievers to a knowledge of spiritual truths.

And there was probably no one more astounded at the spiritual and at the physical results which at first attended the licence afforded to individual experience than Wesley himself. He had learned the art of field preaching from Whitefield, his great contemporary, and had seen 20,000 men and women of all classes, standing in all weathers, to catch echoes of the great preacher's soul-stirring messages. But this had not prepared him for the results that were to follow his own sermons in the cathedral not made with hands. For one day after Wesley had expounded the 4th chapter of the Acts, somebody "called upon God to confirm his word." Immediately first one and then another amongst his listeners, either "cried out with the utmost vehemence, as though in the agonies of death; or were seized with strong pain and constrained to roar for the disquietness of their heart; or fell to the ground in trance, in a state of ecstasy, or were thrown into fits, and seemed to be literally torn by Satan."

A Quaker who was inveighing against what he called the dissimulation of these creatures, was himself caught and struck down as if by lightning. His agony, says Wesley, was terrible to behold: but after Wesley had prayed for him, he lifted up his head and cried aloud, "Now I know thou art a prophet of the Lord."

The worst cases and paroxysms were only recovered by the power of prayer. Wesley, however, was not carried away by these occurrences; he scrutinized them with watchful eye to distinguish true from false, and to discover the cause, but he argues, "I have seen with my own eyes and heard with my ears several things which to the best of my judgment cannot be accounted for by the ordinary course of natural causes, and which I therefore believe ought to be ascribed to the extraordinary interposition of God. If any man choose to call these miracles, I reclaim not. I have weighed the preceding and following circumstances: I have strove to account for them in a natural way: but could not without doing violence to my reason." There is no sign here of hysterical fanaticism in these calmly reasoned words.

These violent phenomena were fortunately discontinued in later years, and Wesley suggests that the reason for their occurrence in early days was that " it might be because of the hardness of our hearts unready to receive anything, unless we see it with our eyes and hear it with our ears, that God in tender condescension to our weakness suffered so many outward signs at the very time when He wrought the inward change, to be continually seen and heard among us."

But that God, " now as aforetime gives remission of sins and the gift of the Holy Ghost, which may be called visions, could not," says Wesley, " be denied. If it be not so I am found a false witness; but, however, I will do and will testify the things I have both seen and heard."

As Wesley reminds his disapproving brother Samuel, " Did not the Gospel promise to us all—to all that are afar off—the witness of God's spirit with their spirit, that they are the children of God ? "

And so, as of old, these signs followed them that believed. Wesley healed the sick and recovered the dying; he exorcised evil spirits as easily as he converted sinners, reclaimed drunkards, and aroused the indifferent. And all, as he believed, by supernatural interposition, or as we to-day call it, by means of supernormal faculties vouchsafed in furtherance of his efforts, by the Spirit of God.

People make much ado to-day about the new discovery of spiritual healing. But Wesley's Journal tells of cures and wonders worked by faith and prayer " designed," as he put it, " by God for the further manifestation of His work, to cause His power to be known, and to awaken the attention of a drowsy world." " It was not," he says, " the work of man which hath lately appeared ; all who calmly observe it must say, ' This is the Lord's doing and it is marvellous in our eyes.'" Why then be surprised and taken aback ?

The Churches, when they found that Wesley was urging men to seek truth in their own hearts rather than in ecclesiastical tradition, shut their doors upon him, as also upon his brother Charles, the hymn-maker, and their great contemporary Whitefield, and drove them out into the fields and hedgerows. But were not the best sermons in the world preached upon a mountain or from a fishing boat upon a lake ?

It is, of course, impossible to explain in so many words the secret of the extraordinary power of Wesley's preaching. This gentlemanly looking, trim little man, with the aquiline nose, clear complexion, and bright piercing eyes, had no great presence, no tricks of oratory, no anecdotes, no humour, very little imagination, and no descriptive power (Fitchett). But as the wind plays upon a field of corn and sways the myriad heads of grain this way and that way as though they were but one, so Wesley swayed and stirred, with the stormy breath of the Spirit speaking through him, the hearts of the multitudes 20,000 to 30,000 at a time, who stood in all weathers under the open sky, in the fields and hedgerows near the cities, or in the rocky amphitheatres of the West, or in the mountains of the North—that they might learn how they, even the humblest amongst them, might find God.

His audiences were composed of men and women of all ages and of all classes, but chiefly of peasants and miners and the rabble of the cities. He preferred preaching to the poor, for it was very hard, he said, to be shallow enough for a polite audience.

But can we suppose that Wesley or any man on earth would have been able during a period of fifty years, to attract and to reach the hearts of these open-air multitudes, had he not himself been convinced by his own personal experience of the truths which he interpreted ? One ounce of conviction is for any speaker worth a ton of oratory.

It is computed that in those fifty years he preached 42,400 sermons, on an average more than fifteen a week, and that he itinerated on horseback, or in later years in carriages, more than 250,000 miles up and down the country.

Wesley married, but the less said about that the better. He married a well-to-do widow, with four children, and concerning her Southey remarks that she deserved to be classed in a triad with Xantippe and the wife of Job, as one of the world's three worst wives. But in justice to her it must be admitted that Wesley, though he was a genius in the art of administrating and organizing religious societies, was a tyro in the more difficult art of husbandry.

Southey tells us, for instance, that, " By right of belonging to the more worthy gender," Wesley thought it appropriate to write in the following terms to the wife of his bosom, she having apparently complained of his neglect : " Be content," he wrote, " to be a private, insignificant person known and loved by God and me. . . . Of what importance is your character to mankind ? If you was buried just now, or if you had never lived, what loss would it be to the cause of God?" And Southey's comment is that this was very true, but not very conciliating.

But a happy married life would have been fatal to Wesley's work, as it proved a hindrance to that of his brother Charles, and has been disastrous to many other would-be workers in God's cause. Nothing short of the whole-hearted, untrammelled, and lifelong devotion of this tireless enthusiast could have enabled him so to impress the world of religious thought as to enable even a secular critic such as Lecky to say that John Wesley's conversion " forms an epoch in English history ; and that the religious revolution begun in England by the preaching of the Wesleys is of greater importance than all the splendid victories by land and sea won under Pitt," and that " Wesley was one of the chief

JOHN WESLEY

forces that saved England from a revolution such as France knew."

The outward and visible result of his work may be gauged by statistics, which in 1901 showed that there were then 48,334 ministers, 104,786 local preachers, 89,087 churches, 7,659,285 members, 81,228 Sunday Schools, 861,392 teachers and officers, 7,077,079 scholars, and 24,899,421 adherents.

Wesley passed to the greater knowledge in 1791, at the age of eighty-seven years, whispering as he passed : " The best of all is, God is with us."

History repeats itself, especially perhaps in matters of religion, and there is an interesting analogy between the relationship of Wesley and his followers to the eighteenth-century Church and the relationship of spiritualists to the Churches of to-day. For Wesley, when explaining to many hundred communicants in Dublin in 1789 the original design of the so-called Methodists, clearly announced that " his followers were not to be a distinct party, but that they were to stir up all parties, Christians and heathens, to worship God in spirit and in truth ; but the Church of England in particular, to which they belonged from the beginning."

And similarly spiritualists to-day have no desire to be a party distinct from the Churches—those institutions in which have been centred the religious sentiments of a lifetime. But the Churches of the twentieth century are closing their doors to those who believe in and who would preach personal revelation and spirit inspiration, as the Churches of the eighteenth century shut their narrow doors against the great religious genius who with tongues of living fire would have restored to the Churches their Pentecostal power.

But at the risk of exclusion from the privileges of fellowship in an old and much-loved Church, Wesley was compelled, as spiritualists are compelled to-day, to preach the wider truth. Wesley knew, as all his great predecessors knew, and as all spiritualists to-day know, that neither submission to Church rules, nor intellectual belief, nor works of piety, can ever bring that inner conviction, that

212 TORCHBEARERS OF SPIRITUALISM

assurance of life beyond the grave, that assurance which links man to Eternity, enhances his self-respect and touches the mainsprings of human conduct.

Like all the other great teachers whose lives we have here sketched, Wesley founded his religion, not upon tradition, but upon knowledge. He first obtained personal knowledge of the world of spirit, and then was led, as all noble minds are led, to advance from the psychic to the spiritual plane, where alone is found that higher knowledge which is Wisdom —the Wisdom of the Great Initiates.

THE CHRIST

WE have left the most delicate and difficult portion of our task until the end, because as it is more important that the world should believe in the truth of the Gospel story than in any of the other stories here recorded, we shall have the benefit of cumulative evidence to help us to accept as Truth, those so-called miracles of the Christian Faith which are a stumbling-block to the thousands of honest people who stay away from church because they cannot believe what the Churches teach.

But have we a right, is it not sacrilege, to include Jesus among the earthly Torchbearers whom we have named? Was not Jesus Divine, the Son of God, and in a category apart? If this were so, if the nature of Jesus differed from that of Man, in the sense signified by the Churches, it would of course serve no purpose here to refer to One who was outside the scope of laws to which the human Initiates were subjected. But have the Churches justification for their assumption of an exclusive Divinity for Jesus? In former years it was considered irreverent even to mention the name of God or of Jesus, except in church, or in a whisper, and it takes even to-day a bold man or woman to discuss in cold print the nature and attributes of these lofty Beings. But since the future of Christianity depends upon whether those who have been born in the Christian Faith can in these days take such a view of the nature and attributes of the Founder of their Faith, that His religion can be a driving force in their lives, it seems worth while to venture upon this dangerous emprise.

Also, the question is of importance to all those Spiritualists who desire to remain within the folds of the Churches in which they have been brought up. For if Spiritualism cannot accept the Divinity of the Christ, Spiritualism must, say the Churches, be placed upon the Index.

Since then this question of the Divinity is crucial both for Spiritualists and for churchmen, it seems worth while to face the difficulty, in the humble hope of paving a way for a union between two bands of workers who are, in their respective ways, both working for spiritual ends. Let us then boldly grasp the nettle.

But may we first ask our readers to free their minds from, possibly, life-long sentiment, and from prejudice, and to approach the subject with the reasoning faculties, realizing that the greater the importance of the subject, the greater is the need to find the truth, whatever it may cost. And may we add this assurance, that the truth as we conceive it, concerning the Divinity of Jesus, is a far more glorious and satisfying possession than the nebulous and incomprehensible doctrine which has been imposed upon us by the Churches.

What then is usually understood by the word " divine " as applied to the Christ ? Now the word " divine " is, like the word Faith, one of those words representing an abstract idea, which it has been very dangerous to let loose in a world peopled with ignorant and prejudiced people. The tendency is always to give the abstract idea concreteness by attaching it to some one objective figure. Words which originally had a generic significance gradually become narrowed to some specific meaning ; they are often attached to a specific Cause, or to a specific person, whilst retaining the glamour and the glory which pertained to their wider meaning.

But we will take the commonly accepted definition of " divine " which is given in our dictionaries to-day. We are there told that the word divine is derived from the Latin " Divus," a deity, and that it signifies " of, or belonging to God or the deity."

Now without entering here into abstruse metaphysics as

THE CHRIST

to the distinction between God and Deity, but taking the word God in its usually accepted sense, as the One God and Father of All, what is that quality or attribute of which we can with any reason predicate that it " belongs to God " ?

It is of course presumption to attempt to talk about what does or what does not belong to God, but speaking in conformity with general usage, we may say that the attribute which par excellence belongs to God, is that of being Spirit. We assume that God is a Spirit, and that as Spirit He called forth, and perhaps literally called forth—as emanations, as materialized thought-forms, the whole Universe, including Man. God, in short, is Spirit, and only Spirit. He is Spirit in excelsis. God is Spirit, or, as far as Man is concerned, He is nothing.

But the Churches teach that Man has a dual nature, and that in addition to being Man, he is also spirit. Now though spirits may differ in degrees of loftiness and of holiness, Spirit is Spirit, and can be referred to no other category. So that when the Churches claim that in addition to his manhood, Man is endowed also with spirithood, they make Man a partaker of the nature of God, and if God is Divine on account of being Spirit, Man must also be Divine on that same account.

And though in respect to his manhood, the nature of Man differs in kind from that of God, yet in respect to his spirithood, the nature of Man differs from that of God only in *degree*. The greater includes the lesser, and if Man is Spirit as well as Man, he is not less a Spirit because he is also Man.

And if it is by virtue of being Spirit that God is said to be Divine, must not Man by virtue of being Spirit, also be Divine ? If this is not so, then the Divineness of God must be based, not upon His spirit-nature, but upon some other nature, and of such other nature we hear nothing from the Churches. The fact that God may, as attributes of a supremely lofty spirit-nature, be all-powerful, all-wise, all-anything-else the Churches may devise, would only again differentiate God from Man in degree, and not in kind, since all such attributes are, in varying degrees of intensity, attainable by Man as Spirit. The possession by God of a thousand other attributes would not minimize the main fact that the nature of God is said to be Spirit. And is it not then reasonable to assume that however inferior in degree Man may be to God, yet that in so far as Man is Spirit, then by virtue of his spirit-nature, he is differentiated from God not at all in kind, but only in degree ? Therefore if God is Divine, Man must also be Divine.

How is it then with Jesus ? In what respect was Jesus Divine in some way unattainable by Man ? The Churches teach that Jesus took our nature upon Him—and by this presumably they mean our human nature. But the Divinity of Jesus is attributed to Him not on account of His human nature, not on account of His manhood, but on account of His Spirithood, and any contention as to the exact means by which He entered either into His human or into His Spirit life is irrelevant to the main issue, which is concerned with the fact, admitted both by the Churches and by Spiritualists, that He was Divine.

But if Jesus was Divine by virtue of being Spirit, has not every man and woman for whom spirithood is claimed, equally the right, according to our showing, to be called Divine ? And is not therefore the differentiation between the divineness of Man and the divineness of Jesus, again one only of degree ? And though the term Divine takes on a deeper meaning when applied to One whose Nature partook more of Spirit than can be claimed for most men, we must not be blinded to the fact that the difference between the spirithood of Jesus and the spirithood of Man, is, according to all logical deductions, one only of degree and not of kind, and that to exaggerate the Spirithood of Jesus to the extent of denying to Man any degree of that Divineness which is inherent in all Spirithood, is to make of Jesus a distinct and isolated species, a species distinct from Man and distinct also from God.

Distinct from Man, since if He was both Man and Spirit, and yet in His Spirithood was something fundamentally apart from anything inherent in the Spirithood of Man,

THE CHRIST

He constituted in Himself a category apart from all human beings, either before or since His life on earth.

But He also then constituted a new and isolated species not only on the earth but in the Heavens. For by virtue of His dual nature He was differentiated from God, who is said to have remained as only Spirit, from everlasting. Thus by those who claim for Jesus—as contrasted with Man—this attribute of an exclusive Divinity, Jesus must be regarded as a species apart from all Beings, human or spiritual, of whom the world has record. Or—as the only and miserable alternative, we are dragged into the confused and hairsplitting metaphysics of the Athanasian Creed.

Now the logomachy of such Creeds may have been tolerable in times when the word Spirit had no objective meaning, when it was merely, like the blessed word Mesopotamia, a vague abstraction which for would-be religious minds called up fancy pictures of harps and golden crowns. It is perhaps good enough also for those who, following the lead of our Churches and of our dictionaries, still regard the words soul and spirit as synonymous terms. But to those who have come in personal contact with Spirit, and who are —all humbly—learning to understand the objectivity of Spirit, as a reality here and now, the metaphysics of the Churches cuts no ice. No one to-day is brought nearer to God by recitation of the Athanasian Creed.

There were days when it was taken for granted that Man could not expect to understand things pertaining to the Spirit. Man's understanding, whilst on earth, was supposed to be finite, and incapable of apperceiving the Infinite. He must therefore leave the Infinite alone and be content with any sentimental vagaries which the Churches might impose upon him. The fact that Man has a dual nature here and now, that he is not Man now and Spirit hereafter, but that he is Man and Spirit *here and now*, was ignored. It was therefore also ignored that as Spirit, Man might, if he attuned himself to spiritual conditions, gain some understanding, at least some inkling, of spiritual verities.

And to-day, for many thousands of intellectual people,

the word Spirit is not a far-away metaphysical abstraction, beyond the comprehension of mundane minds. Spiritualists know to-day from personal experience that Spirit is a concrete reality which can be scientifically studied in laboratories.

It is perhaps natural that when difference in degree is great, men are apt to drift into assuming difference in kind ; and in some classes of animal life it is true that excessive differences in degree may lead to a new type. But we are not here faced with any such complication. If God is Divine by virtue of being Spirit—and we only know of Him as Spirit—then it was by virtue of being Spirit that Jesus was Divine, and it is by virtue of this same, that Man is Divine.

What the Churches have done is to exaggerate the Spirithood, the Divinity of Jesus, and to minimize the spirithood, the Divinity of Man, to such an extent as to have blinded the world to a recognition of the Divinity of Man, and to have created a barrier, an artificial barrier, between Man and Jesus, between Man and God. And when the Churches accuse Spiritualists of denying the Divinity of Jesus, there is but one reply. The Spiritualists do not deny the Divinity of Jesus, any more than they deny the Divinity of God. But they demand that the Divinity of Man shall also be recognized.

And if the Divinity of Man is acknowledged, then it is only a question of degree between the Divinity of One who, when on earth, allowed His Spirithood rather than His Manhood to preponderate, and the Divinity of those who, encouraged by their Churches to believe that they are conceived and born in sin, and that there is no health—no spiritual health—in them, have allowed their human nature to prevail over their spirit-nature, to such an extent, that in the majority of people the functions of the Spirit have become atrophied and the power of functioning on the spirit-plane is wellnigh lost.

Man's recognition of his power of functioning as Spirit, as well as of his power of functioning as Man, can only be **regained through exercising** his psychic faculties—those

THE CHRIST

faculties through which alone Spirit is able to function on this earth. For as the body functions by means of the physical, and the mind by means of the intellectual faculties, so it is by means of the psychic faculties that the soul of Man can function.

The Churches acknowledge that they are a decaying force. Can the clergy not see that Spiritualism is the tonic which would restore life and vigour to their now anæmic Church ? Can they not realize that Religion is not Morality, or Theology, or Ritual, or Worship, but Revelation, and that Revelation has been obtained in all ages and in all countries, by means of the psychic faculty, and by means of the psychic faculty alone.

If then by the Divinity of Jesus is meant an attribute which Jesus shared, and in superlative degree, with all mankind, He, together with all those who were " made in the image of God," was divine, and more gloriously divine than the rest of mankind. But if by this term is signified a quality possessed by the Christ alone, a quality which isolates Him from the whole scheme of natural law as exemplified elsewhere in the Universe, then for such a startling belief, we must ask for stronger evidence than that afforded by the Churches.

And it is not, we think, a travesty of the orthodox view to say that by Christ's Divinity the Churches signify an attribute which differentiates Him from every other living being born upon the earth ; that for the Churches, Christ's Divinity implies that He was, in a more than poetic sense, the Son of God ; that He was born of a woman, and was in this respect human, but that He was conceived by a Spirit,—the Holy Ghost, the third Person of the Trinity,— and was in this respect Divine.

Now to find a parallel to this crude and materialistic view of the intervention of spirits in this branch of human affairs, we must turn to the 6th chapter of Genesis. Here we find that at a time when there was general ignorance as to how procreation was effected, men attributed it to direct spirit intervention ; and we are told that the sons of God, that is, spirits from another plane, "took them wives of the daughters of men," and that these daughters "bare children to them"—the spirits. The children were thus presumed to have been born without the participation of the human male. In other words, the functions of earthly fatherhood were not understood, and though for obvious reasons it was impossible to doubt the mother's share of responsibility in the birth of the child, the share contributed by the man was unrecognized.

And so we read that when Cain was born, Eve, in innocence of how he had been conceived, declared : "I have gotten a man from the Lord" (Gen. iv. 1). Or, as the Revised Version translates it, in a brave effort to adapt the idea to more modern knowledge, "I have gotten a man with the help of the Lord."

In these days of general knowledge on the subject, and when methods even of birth control are openly discussed, the naïveté of those early days seems almost incredible. But in the custom of the Couvade we meet with similar ignorance. For, in obedience with this custom, when the child was born, the man, piqued lest it should be felt that he had had no share in the production of the child, went to bed and feigned sickness, whilst the woman waited upon him.

This custom prevailed in Burmah, and it is said still to exist in Biscay, and to be common in Yunnan and among the Miris in Upper Assam. Also among the Caribs of the West Indies, the Abipones of Central South America, the Aborigines of California, in Guiana, in West Africa, and in the Indian Archipelago. It is said to have existed at one time in Corsica and in the North of Spain, and Apollonius Rhodius tells us that " In the Tabarenian land (on the Euxine Sea) :—

> When some good woman bears her lord a babe,
> 'Tis he is swathed and groaning put to bed :
> While she arising tends his bath and serves
> Nice Possets for her husband in the straw.[1]

---

[1] Argonautic Exp. (*The Readers' Handbook*).

THE CHRIST

The doctrine, therefore, of the Church, that Christ was divine because he was the Son of God, and that He was the Son of God mainly by virtue of His conception by the Holy Ghost, would seem to be a reversion to an ancient superstition which was based upon ignorance of physiological laws.

Is it worthy of the dignity, of the reverence which should be attached to all the events in the Life of the Christ, to make these superstitious assumptions as to His origin and the manner of His birth?

But we would further ask what authority have the Churches for this doctrine of the Virgin Birth and Holy Ghost conception? Do the Churches claim any other authority than that of the Bible? But where in the Bible is there justification for the founding of what is said to be a fundamental doctrine of the Christian Church?

The story of the miraculous birth is given only by Matthew and by Luke; it is not mentioned by Mark, from whom Matthew and Luke are said to have derived their main source of inspiration; nor by John, who, as the specially beloved disciple, would have been likely to have known as much about his Master as anyone. Is it not reasonable to suppose that if belief in the miraculous birth had been at that time at all general, that Mark and John, as also Paul, would have made use of this as the basis of their exhortations to belief in Christ?

The Churches, then, are dependent upon the stories of the birth told by Matthew and by Luke. But these stories differ so materially from each other that it is difficult for the lay mind to understand how both accounts could be supposed to have been inspired or how both could possibly have been true. And if only one of these two versions is correct, why has the Church selected that of Matthew rather than that of Luke as the origin and foundation of one of its main tenets?

Still more difficult is it to understand how from either of these contradictory stories the Churches can have based authoritative doctrines considered to be of vital importance for those who would be members of the Church. For according to Matthew, the Angel of the Lord appeared to Joseph *after the conception,* and told him that the child that would be born to Mary had been conceived by the Holy Ghost; whereas in Luke's version of the birth, the Angel appeared to *Mary before* the conception, and tells her, not that she will conceive by the Holy Ghost, but that she will conceive and bring forth a son who will be great and who will be *called* the Son of the Highest. The Angel does not say, he will be the Son of the Highest.

And then in response to Mary's question as to how this could all be, the Angel tells her that the Holy Ghost will come upon her and will overshadow her, and that therefore that Holy Thing which will be born of her will be *called* the Son of God.

Here, therefore, we have two distinct theories presented by Matthew and by Luke respectively. The former assumes the ancient superstition of direct conception by a Spirit from another plane; whilst Luke—the physician, who had presumably a more up-to-date knowledge of physiological laws—merely suggests that a Holy Spirit would overshadow Mary.

And this latter is in conformity with a belief which was then prevalent and which was distinct from and had presumably superseded the more ancient superstition: a belief which is indeed held by many to-day—the belief, namely, that the spirits of those who had passed could control and influence the lives of those on earth.

Luke records, in conformity with this view, that about this same time Mary's cousins, Zacharias and Elizabeth, were similarly visited by an angel of the Lord—by the much over-worked Gabriel—who foretold to them also the birth of a child, John the Baptist, who would be filled with the Holy Ghost, the Holy Spirit, even from his mother's womb (Luke i.). This child was to be filled with the spirit and power of Elijah, but no one has ever suggested that Elijah was the father of John the Baptist.

Indeed, this phrase " to be filled with the Holy Ghost " was commonly used to signify that the person of whom the words were spoken was possessed of the prophetic, that is, of the psychic gift. Elizabeth was " filled with the Holy Ghost " when she foretold to Mary clairvoyantly before Jesus was born, that she would be the mother of the long-expected prophet, the Lord.

Zacharias also is said to have been " filled with the Holy Ghost" when he prophesied in the words of the Benedictus " Blessed be the Lord, the God of Israel," etc.

But it is evident from both Matthew's and from Luke's versions of the story, that there seemed to be nothing that was unusual about the appearance of the Angel or his reference to the Holy Spirit, and if, as seems likely, the salient feature in both accounts was the appearance of an angel, of a spirit, who prophesied that Mary's child would be filled, or influenced to an unusual degree, by a Holy Spirit, this would account for the fact that the story seemed of so little importance to Mark, and to John, that it was never even referred to by them.

Further, there is nowhere in the Gospels a hint that the contemporaries of Christ were aware of anything miraculous about his birth. On the contrary, in Nazareth, in the village where he had been brought up, and where all his family story must have been well known, when he entered into the synagogue and by his exposition of the Scriptures astonished his hearers, " they wondered at the words of grace which proceeded out of his mouth, and they said: ' Is not this Joseph's son ? ' " (Luke x. 22).

Again, Nicodemus assumed that Jesus was a *Teacher* come from God, for no man, he said, can do the signs that thou doest, except God be with him." But not as his physical father.

Luke certainly has no idea of presenting Jesus as a miraculously conceived Son of God. On the contrary, after telling us in chapter 3, verse 23, that Jesus was about thirty years of age when he began his ministry, he takes care to give us an elaborate genealogy of Christ's human progenitors: a genealogy which stretches in an unbroken line from " Jesus, being as supposed, the Son of Joseph, which was the son of Heli," all the way back to " Adam, which was the son of God." It is not Jesus, but Adam who is called the son of God, and this doubtless in deference to the old superstition of Adamic days, to which we have referred.

A great deal might be said also concerning these words "Son of God" as used in the New Testament. Paul's understanding of this phrase certainly does not imply any sense of the exclusive sonship of Jesus to the Father of All. For in Romans viii. 14 he says, " For as many as are led by the Spirit of God, these are the sons of God."

There is also another sense in which the appellation Son of God was often used. We have the authority of St. Yves d'Alveydre[1] and others for the fact that in the days when there were four degrees of initiation into the Sacred Mysteries, that those who attained the second degree were called the Sons of man, and that it was reserved for those who reached the fourth and highest degree, to be called the Sons of God. And in this respect the Christ was doubtless recognized to be, as he verily was, the Son of God in a sense that was unique.

But this is a uniqueness of degree and not of kind, and it is to us more inspiring to be able to regard the Christ as having belonged wholly and not with only half his nature to our race of human beings; as one who, though he was specially endowed with the faculty of receiving revelation from the highest source, and though he combined to an exceptional degree the moral, psychic, and spiritual qualities essential in a religious genius, yet was in very truth the hope of our own resurrection from the dead. For if Christ was himself partly God, in some way which must for ever be impossible to us, the fact that He rose from the dead would be no proof that we who are only human shall similarly rise from the dead, as it is inappropriately termed; we can only derive hope and comfort from the resurrection of

[1] *Mission des Juifs*, pp. 223-24.

THE CHRIST

Christ, if Christ, like us was human, and if there was in His survival of bodily death no contravention of natural laws—laws which in our own case would not be suspended.

In so far, therefore, as belief in the Divinity of Christ is founded upon the New Testament accounts of his birth, we find it difficult to find in these two accounts warrant for such a startling belief. The discrepancy between the two is indeed so great that we can only wisely accept that wherein they both agree, and that is the fact that the Nature of Christ was to a great extent determined by pre-natal spirit influences of a high order, and that the psychic conditions preceding His birth—whether they were the immediate experience of Joseph or of Mary—helped to create for Jesus in His home life a psychic and a spiritual atmosphere helpful in fostering His own great powers.

We do not propose here to deal with the various events in the life of the Christ which are supposed by the Churches to be of a miraculous nature, of a character which was unique and supernatural, and which differentiated Jesus from all other men. We have dealt with them in detail elsewhere.[1]

And readers who will take the trouble to compare these main events in the life of the world's greatest and noblest bearer of the Torch of Truth, with events which we have recorded in the lives of the lesser Torchbearers, will have no difficulty in realizing that the basic features of the Christian Religion, those events which have been regarded by the Churches as affording evidence, in the Christ, of a nature that was supernatural and unique, those events are closely paralleled in the lives of the Torchbearers we have named. And further, students of psychic science will observe that these occurrences are in conformity with phenomena which are taking place to-day, and which can be verified by scientific researchers; that they belong therefore to a category which is neither supernatural nor unique. The Christ's works of healing were conducted upon lines which are well understood and which are successfully practised to-day; the Transfiguration, the so-called Resur-

[1] *Ancient Lights.*

rection, the post-resurrection appearances, and the Ascension, though all on a scale of sublimity that has never been equalled, present no features which are unfamiliar to modern students of psychic science. They were neither supernatural nor unique, they were of a nature which entitles us to look with human pride and gratitude to Jesus as an example of what could be achieved by lifelong training and self-sacrifice, and by a rare and balanced combination of psychic, spiritual, and moral qualities.

Incidentally also, in pursuance of one of our main arguments, is it not as true of Jesus, as of the lesser Torchbearers in our series, that but for the events in His life which partook of a supernormal, but not supernatural nature, we should never have known of the Saviour. But for His signs and wonders, His so-called miracles, and His works of healing, the multitude would have paid no heed to His preaching. And but for His mis-named Resurrection, His post-resurrection appearances, and His Ascension, Christianity would have died upon the Cross.

The disciples, and above all Paul, concerned themselves almost exclusively after Christ's death, in preaching " Christ risen from the dead." " If Christ is not risen, then is your faith vain," etc. And if " Christ risen " had not been for those disciples, those ignorant fisher folk, a reality which they had seen with their own eyes, they would have had no gospel to preach.

And as we know from the story of St. Thomas, and from the incredulity of the eleven apostles, when Mary Magdalene, Joanna, and Mary the mother of James, told them what they had seen at the tomb, these things appeared in the sight of the apostles as " idle talk " till they saw these things with their own eyes. They were not therefore more credulous or more easily convinced of the genuineness of unfamiliar phenomena, than are most people to-day.

Now we shall doubtless be, by the orthodox, condemned as irreverent for treating the Christ in the same category with these preceding Initiates. But can we only reverence the great by isolating them and crediting them with qualities

THE CHRIST

of uniqueness which make them incomprehensible ? The very essence of Christ's teaching was that it and He Himself should be within the reach of all. As Moses centuries before had brought the sacred Mysteries and the knowledge of a universal Deity out of the temples and given them into the guardianship of the Hebrew people : so Christ, in even more universal spirit, brought the knowledge of God the Father and of eternal life into the hearts of every man, woman, and child who willed to receive it.

Christ's preaching was, as Paul tells us (Rom. xvi. 25), " According to the revelation of the Mystery which hath been kept in silence through times eternal, *but now is manifested,*" and we believe that it is in keeping with the spirit of Christ's teaching that it shall be manifest to all. And this can only be brought about by an understanding of the phenomena by means of which Christ enforced His teaching.

We suggest that if the Churches would, for instance, make themselves acquainted with the *modus operandi* of those metapsychic laws in accordance with which Christ's Transfiguration, Resurrection, and Ascension were effected, they would be able to bring the truth of these events home to the heart and understanding both of the learned and of the simple : they would speak from conviction, and therefore with power, and religion would be revolutionized.

If they would take the trouble to discover—and they are discoverable—the methods by which Christ and His disciples healed the sick and exorcised evil, they would have no cause to complain of empty churches : the healing of sick bodies and the restoration to spiritual health of sick souls are, as Christ knew, processes which are interdependent, but they are effected not by means of asserting faith in supernatural myths, but by the attainment of a simple and spiritual wisdom which is obtained from the one and only source of wisdom.

And now if we are to treat the Christ as a great human Brother and an Initiate of the highest and rarest Order, is it legitimate to wonder where and how He obtained His training and His occult wisdom ? And in answering this question we at once link up the greatest of all Initiates with those predecessors whose lives we have outlined. For according to Schuré, who does not speak without authority, there is reason to believe that Jesus spent those years of His early life before His ministry, years of which in the Gospels we have no record, serving a long period of initiation in the sacred Mysteries, with the Order of the Essenians, an ascetic sect who, scattered in groups over Palestine and Egypt, were the last of the Brotherhood of the Prophets organized by Samuel (*Les Grands Initiés*).

It was doubtless from these Essenians, whose chief public mission was the healing of physical and of moral sickness by methods of which they had made a special study, that Jesus learnt the secrets of His great healing power : from their custom of communal repasts that He derived His Sacramental Supper : from their Cup of final Initiation, which contained " the wine of the true vine of the Lord," his Communion Cup of the Last Supper : and it was therefore probably in common with the Essenians that Jesus practised celibacy, community of goods, free hospitality to brethren of the Order : that He taught love of neighbour, humility, prohibition to take oath : and that He wore linen garments. From them it was, in short, that he derived much of that esoteric wisdom that they had inherited in direct line from Pythagoras, from Orpheus, and from Krishna. In short, it was with these exemplary, moral, and occultly learned Essenians that He initiated, and that He then attained both to the second degree, and became as He called Himself a " Son of Man," and also to the highest degree and became a " Son of God."

If this be true—and if it be not true we might well ask with His fellow-countrymen, " Whence hath this man this knowledge and this wisdom ? "—if this be true, then the Christ and His teaching are definitely linked in an historic chain with the great Teachers and Initiates of all time.

And if this be so, then evidence for the veridical nature of the supernormal events in the life of Christ is cumulative —through the Ages—and unless we reject the supernormal,

THE CHRIST

that is the psychic element in the stories of all those whose lives we have outlined, we are justified in concluding that all Religion—even the Religion of the Christ—has been obtained by means of Revelation, and that Revelation has in all cases been acquired by means of the psychic faculty.

Also that the Truths taught by the World's Great Teachers, namely, the existence of God, the dual nature of Man, and Man's survival of bodily death, have always been the same, and that they have been the same because they have been derived by revelation from the same source.

Therefore in acknowledging Christ, we are more than Christians, we are followers of Plato, of Pythagoras, of Rama. But we are hindered from seeing this, we are hindered from realizing the vastness, the agelong character of our religious heritage, because the Churches, in accentuating the Divinity of Christ, have estranged us from a consciousness of the Divinity inherent in every man who is " in the image of God."

We, however, know to-day that though one planet differeth from another, this is in magnitude only and not in kind. They are all linked as interdependent units in a gravitational Whole, in obedience to the same laws, and all derive their substance and their light from the same great Central Sun. And as the study of the Heavens became a stimulating science when the more comprehensive knowledge of Copernicus supplanted the old belief that the sun and all the universe revolved around our Earth, so will the study of Religion become a glorious and absorbing science, when men realize that Revelation has not been restricted within the narrow orbit prescribed by the doctrines of the Church, but that Revelation is the Breath of God broadcasted through the Universe in accents which can be understood by all those who, like the Great Initiates, attune their souls to catch sounds from the Divine.

BIBLIOGRAPHY

I SHOULD like it to be understood that though I am responsible for opinions and for deductions from the facts recorded in this volume, I have derived my information from the following—amongst other books—from which I have unrestrainedly extracted all that seemed helpful to my purpose. I therefore desire to acknowledge my indebtedness and to proffer to these various authors, on their various planes, a humble avowal of my dependence upon their original and valuable researches.

G. G. ALEXANDER : Lao-Tzû the Great Thinker.
JAMES ADAM : The Religious Teachers of Greece.
BICKLEY'S Life of George Fox and the Early Quakers.
G. G. ALEXANDER : Confucius.
R. NICOLL CROSS : Socrates the Man and his Mission.
CONYBEARE'S translation of Philostratus's Life of Apollonius.
RHYS DAVIDS : Buddhism.
MOHINI M. DHAR : Krishna the Charioteer.
R. R. DOUGLAS : Confucianism and Taoism.
A. CONAN DOYLE'S translation of Léon Denis's " Mystery of Joan of Arc."
H. G. DAKYNS : The Works of Xenophon.
DESERTIS : Psychic Philosophy.
Encyclopedia Britannica.
EUCKEN : The Truth of Religion.
EMERSON : Representative Men.
FABRE D'OLIVET : La Langue Hébraique restituée.
FABRE D'OLIVET : Hermeneutic Interpretation of the Origin of the Social State of Man.
FITCHETT : Wesley and his Century.
GOMPERTZ (transl. by G. G. Berry) : Greek Thinkers.
GILES : Selections from Chuang Tzû.

BIBLIOGRAPHY 231

GILES: Religions of Ancient China.
GILES (transl.): Chuang Tzû.
G. CUNNINGHAME GRAHAM: Santa Teresa.
HOWITT: Supernaturalism in All Ages.
W. R. INGE: The Philosophy of Plotinus.
DIOGENES LAERTIUS: Lives of the Philosophers.
ANDREW LANG: Story of Joan of Arc.
T. TAYLOR (transl.), edited G. H. MEAD: Plotinus.
G. R. S. MEAD: Fragments of a Faith Forgotten.
G. R. S. MEAD: Quests Old and New.
G. R. S. MEAD: Apollonius of Tyana.
ISABELLA MEARS' translation of the Tao-teh-King.
W. MUIR: The Life of Mohammed.
OUSPENSKY: Tertium Organum.
PLATO's Dialogues.
ED. SCHURÉ: Les Grands Initiés.
ST. YVES D'ALVEYDRE: Mission des Juifs.
JULES SIMON: L'histoire de l'École d'Alexandrie.
R. SHIRLEY: Occultists and Mystics of All Ages.
ST. HILAIRE: The Buddha and His Religion.
BERNARD SHAW: St. Joan.
A. SPRENGER: The Life of Mohammed.
M. A. STOBART: Ancient Lights.
SALE: The Koran.
SOUTHEY: Life of WESLEY.
G. TAYLOR: Varia Socratica.
G. TROBRIDGE: Life of Emanuel Swedenborg.
L. TYERMAN: Life and Times of the Rev. S. Wesley.
CHAS. WHITBY: The Wisdom of Plotinus.
WESLEY'S Journal.
J. J. WILKINSON: Emanuel Swedenborg.